THE SILENT THOUGHT

AMERICA IN TRANSITION AND CRISIS

CHARLIE WURZ

The Silent Thought
Copyright © 2022 by Charlie Wurz

03.11.22

TABLE OF CONTENTS

PREFACE

Silent thought!

What is it? And what do we do about it?

When I wrote my first book, *The Silent Thought: America in Crisis*, I started it with this very question. I then followed that question with my explanation for writing that book by making the following statements.

> My reason for writing this book is rooted in my determination to understand what promotes thought, or the lack of thought altogether, and why thought does not progress to expression in either word or action.
>
> Then to examine how this interconnects with a variety of challenges facing our nation, challenges, which I believed to be in a state of crisis, which I now believe to be in even greater crisis after the 2020 presidential election.

My determination has only strengthened, and I am convinced that the concept of silent thought affects many in America and their ability to think critically about the crises I discuss in this book.

The subtitle *America in Transition and Crisis* speaks to the transition period and crises we find in today's America.

Over time, we have moved through several transitional periods. Two world wars and the Great Depression in the twentieth century as well as the American Civil War in the nineteenth century are examples.

I believe that as we entered the twenty-first century, our current state of transition was triggered by the 9/11 attack. As we progressed forward through the twenty years of President's Bush, Obama and Trump, America experienced many challenges, with each president making choices that have taken our nation in several directions of great concern.

I wrote my first book in the lead-up to the 2016 presidential election and now post-presidential election 2020, I see a nation in transition facing serious challenges (crises) but also a nation very divided based on many different viewpoints.

I published this book, "The Silent Thought, America in Transition and Crisis, in 2017. After the 2020 presidential results, I decided to update this book, but waited until President Biden concluded his first year in office.

I do not need to wait any longer to start writing this update, as it is very clear through the great quantity of executive orders and statements by President Biden as to which direction, he and his administration wish to take this country. Much more on Biden in later chapters.

I also find myself writing this book after we commemorated the twenty-year anniversary of the 9/11 attack in Biden's first year, which really brings perspective to this update.

I believe and am very concerned that America has never been more divided, which can only lead to destabilization of this great nation!

This transition is not only where we find ourselves after Presidents' Bush, Obama, and Trump to President Biden, but also the transition as it relates to faith, our nation's sovereignty, personal freedoms, societal norms, foreign intervention, terrorism, and then, which direction our country will take to finally solve these crises.

Without national unity, we cannot choose the correct path forward and continue America's greatness!

So, with this transition in mind, when we consider what silent thought is, it is important to see the implications of taking or not taking a thought to verbal expression or action.

Think of all the great improvements to our quality of life and whether these would have been possible if our thoughts were not articulated or acted on, resulting in a variety of positive changes in our daily lives. Conversely, examine how lack of correct thought or having incorrect thought has had adverse effects on human lives.

While silent thought can affect many aspects of our lives, including family, work, social relationships, and so forth, I prefer to examine how silent thought affects the five crises I cite throughout this book.

One crisis, politics in America, demands our full attention as it not only affects the other crises cited in this book but also plays a vital role in shaping the road map this nation will follow. The following concepts I explore in this book:

- Why do many people ignore thoughts regarding politics and instead accept sound bites from others to form their opinions?
- Does the American political system exploit silent thought?
- Is silent thought found in all segments of American society?
- What can be done to promote more thought and expression?
- Who benefits the most or the least from silent thought?

We have reached a critical crossroads in the American way of life; as the 2000, 2008, 2016 and 2020 presidential election results will have profound consequences and are important events in working through this transition. These events encouraged me to write this book and hopefully inspire people to reexamine their thought processes and their resulting expressions and actions.

I write this book as a discussion with the reader to provoke thought and promote a better understanding and perspective on how interconnected our daily lives are with the crises I discuss in the following chapters.

I will not cite countless statistics or the comments of others. My hope is that this book will prompt readers to search out relevant data to either support or refute my assertions and then form their own thoughtful and analytical opinions, no longer casually accepting the opinions of others, and resisting the tendency of silent thought.

I am very concerned that many younger Americans, perhaps the so-called millennials, let's say those born between 1981 and 1994, might take the greatness of this nation for granted, meaning they might think our way of life is so rooted that it is there forever.

This could also be true for some in generation X, those born between 1965 and 1980. This segment might be working toward their goals, building families, identifying with a political ideology, and accepting the status quo.

Some in my generation, baby boomers, those born between 1946 and 1964 and older, accept the status quo as well and might also believe there is insufficient time left for them to effect any change.

They might also believe that they have accomplished their goals, accepted the status quo, and looking toward or enjoying retirement. They might be choosing to let younger generations deal with it.

Certainly, generation Z, those born between 1995 and 2010 play a vital role in understanding these crises and transition facing our nation and our path forward. They also may be the most at risk by those trying to target their thoughts with distortions about the greatness of our country.

I make these assertions with concern, not criticism.

I encourage all of us to stay involved in the political process. The single greatest action every American can take is to vote—but most importantly, vote as a well-informed citizen!

Then most importantly, after a major election such as that of a US president, evaluate our vote as to whether we voted independently or simply followed the desire of others. If not, we will never challenge or validate our thought process.

I believe our younger generations are in the best position to propel the changes we need now in America. Not to mention, they have the most at stake as they start or are in the early and middle stages of their journeys through life. However, they can be the most distracted.

Many Americans seem to be more interested in *House of Cards*, a former fictional television series, rather than our actual political system and its dysfunction.

At times, we all fail to identify the warning signs, which are more disguised now than ever before in our country. All of us should realize that America's greatness and future has never been at greater risk, for many reasons that we will discuss in detail throughout this book.

My greatest hope is that this book will reach the many Americans who have never considered thought in the way I will explain it, and all too often just accept everything as it is.

The first three chapters deal with spontaneous thought, targeted thought, and stubborn thought, providing examples of each and how the concept of silent thought interconnects within all three. In chapters 4 through 8, I talk about several crises currently facing America and discuss how silent thought can have a negative influence on these major challenges facing every American. Those crises are the following:

- Leadership in America
- Political correctness
- Race relations in America
- Politics in America
- Open borders and immigration

I will also discuss the transition that America now finds itself in, not just due to the 2020 election results, but just as important, the effects of Presidents' Bush, Obama, and Trump years in office.

Throughout this book, I also provide alternatives and solutions to combat the negative consequences of silent thought.

I want to stress that I have not written this book from any specific political perspective, such as any political party—Democrat, Republican, liberal, libertarian, conservative, or any other affiliation. Rather, I have written this book from an American perspective, in a very simple and straightforward approach.

Silent thought can be either a choice to not think about a topic at all or a choice to accept a narrow opinion and not apply any critical thought to the topic or simply refuse to consider other viewpoints, especially when considering topics such as politics.

This occurs when adopting a sound bite that may sound very convincing, depending on your perspective, but lacks any critical analysis.

Let's face it, the average citizen finds politics to be boring and not worth the time to worry about, and many feel ?

It will never change, so why worry about it when they can engage in so many other enjoyable topics and activities?

Politicians know this and certainly exploit this apathy by taking advantage of silent thought and then by targeting our thought with their agendas, which may or may not be in our best interest.

If we simply accept their points of view without any critical thought and analysis, we are choosing to sit on the sidelines. This will only continue and worsen until we decide as a unified country to change our political system.

So, who benefits the most and least without a change of course is obvious, is it not!

Our American political system exploits silent thought and the lack of desire by a majority in this country who just don't feel the need to participate in our political system other than voting, sometimes not voting at all, other times only voting in a national presidential election, or vice versa, in a local contest or referendum, and never really noticing a national political contest.

Sure, many of us complain about politics and politicians all the time, but what are we doing other than just that? The solutions are not easy, and it is simpler to just send these concerns to the brain's silent thought chamber and move on.

Silent thought is found in all walks of life, irrespective of your education level, financial situation, political party affiliation, or age. However, it appears in varying degrees within these segments.

Please remember that just because someone is a politician at the highest level of government does not mean he or she is someone of great intelligence. In many cases, it is just the opposite. Never assume that a politician is smarter than you, the American public.

In fact, politicians' incompetence and arrogance have not only caused these crises but also pushed the solutions further from reach! These so-called political leaders in Washington, DC, are failing America and continue to place the future of this great nation in jeopardy.

They practice divisive tactics and engage in political rope-a-dope, which I will discuss in more detail in a later chapter.

The solutions to solving these crises reside in the strength of every American, not in our local and national politicians who, as you will see, have no interest in facing these challenges.

We must now face the dysfunction in Washington, DC, and that of our national politicians and not succumb to the tendency to think it cannot be changed or something or someone else will correct this problem. There are straight-forward solutions, which I will discuss in much greater detail in a later chapter!

My strongest desire is that America become a nation of leaders and then, as leaders, reestablish the greatness of America and all its citizens.

The 2016 presidential election results may have been the first step in igniting this sense of national leadership among its citizenry as Hillary Clinton winning the presidency was supposed to be a foregone conclusion.

However, many in America took this choice very seriously and demonstrated that the Clinton campaign and Washington establishment were completely out of touch with a majority of America.

Yes, I realize Clinton won the popular vote and was widely claimed by many Democrats and many in the media as somehow relevant, which was only a distraction and conveniently overlooked the broad support for Donald Trump across our nation!

I will discuss this in more detail in a later chapter.

I hope my readers find this book to be a quick read and one that stimulates their thought processes in ways that they may have not considered before.

I am not sure if this book should be considered an update of my first and second books or simply my next book, probably a bit of both.

So, let's begin—and please keep an open mind, as the country we all love is in a period of great transition and at serious risk, and we must all be active participants!

CHAPTER 1

Spontaneous Thought

How many ways can silent thought be described? Many! Let's start with the spontaneous thoughts that enter our brain. We briefly think about them, and they often exit our brain very quickly. This could be considered daydreaming or could be some of the most important thoughts of our lives and potentially influence the people closely tied to our individual lives.

Oftentimes we ask ourselves what that last thought was. *I know it had something to do with X, but I cannot remember it fully.* These occasions can be very frustrating, because we think, *Wow! That was really enlightening,* but we just can't remember its entire value.

What I will not do in this book is attempt to be technical about our brain's complicated design and how it processes thought. I will try to talk about everyday experiences and how valuable our thought process is to our daily journey from the time we wake until we fall asleep. Thought during sleep is a totally different process.

How many times have you noticed how fleeting thought can be? It can be very frustrating, with distraction after distraction taking us from one thought to another, and we are sometimes not able to remember what might have been a very valuable thought.

Writing this book is very challenging because as I write each word, sentence, and paragraph, I am constantly thinking about what I am writing as well as all the other daily facets of my life, including family, work, goals, and on and on. I cannot even imagine how many spontaneous thoughts one has in the course of a day. I am sure the professionals in this field may have an idea, and it must be substantial. We have to ask ourselves how one makes it through the workday, irrespective of what we do in the workplace, with all these distractions.

Spontaneous thought can be problematic if it is allowed to consume our day and not allow us to focus on the critical thought needed in order to perform at all levels in the workplace, home, family, and social settings.

Have you ever sat in a coffee shop for any period of time and realized how many different thoughts you experience as you interact silently with other people and their actions or appearances? If you are sitting or standing close enough to hear others speaking—not eavesdropping, just casual instances of overhearing others—you receive even more thought triggers, continuously causing you to have spontaneous thoughts, either very quickly leaving your consciousness or taking more of your thinking and consideration.

This same experience can happen during a business meeting, riding the subway or bus, driving, sitting, or walking in a park, playing a round of golf, or just about everywhere.

So, what do we do about this as we navigate through our day? Do we consider these thought triggers as a nuisance and a distraction, or do we enjoy the stimulus they produce inside of our brains, resulting in all sorts of analysis, certainly not scientific in most cases?

I guess this is the idea behind people watching and the reason we do it, some more than others.

How many different thoughts have you just had while reading the last several paragraphs in this book? I hope they were positive and encouraged you to keep reading.

Ask yourself:

- What benefit can be derived from spontaneous thought?
- Is this innocent curiosity, or are we just nosy?
- Do we form opinions from any of these spontaneous thoughts?

I will give you my answers to these questions.

To fully understand what causes silent thought, we certainly need to experience spontaneous thought so we can experience the benefits derived from spontaneous interactions of thought and analysis.

I believe this is just innocent curiosity, and with just a little inquisitiveness (possibly being nosy), it can expose us to the many great facets of our human existence.

Most definitely, we form opinions from these spontaneous thoughts. These opinions can have a wide range of importance, from insignificant to opinions that have a significant impact on our lives and that of every other person we encounter.

One trigger I have not mentioned, but probably most influences spontaneous thought, is the media impact to our thought process. This comes at us in many forms, such as print, television (both cable and broadcast), internet via news and blog sites, social sites, radio, and advertising of all types.

Let's first think about the media in terms of the so-called main-stream media outlets, such as the major network news channels.

Then let's consider the media and its behavior in the lead-up and aftermath of the 2016 and 2020 presidential elections.

Ask yourself:

- Do we get unbiased news of the day or opinions?
- Should we rely solely on these?
- Are the news anchors presenting unfiltered news, or are they following an agenda, whether that agenda be personal or driven by network executives?
- More specifically, are these news presenters more concerned with their own personal ambitions, including political or social agendas, or are they simply there to inform the public with factual news accounts?
- Have many in the mainstream media news outlets chosen one political perspective over others and report only biased news accounts?

If you are old enough, you can recall when the major networks, NBC, CBS, ABC and their local affiliate stations were the primary aired news sources for the American public. We now have an abundance of cable broadcasts and internet sites that provide many choices for our news consumption.

These sources can be found in many forms, including factual news, opinion talk shows, and internet forums. Unfortunately, many so-called news sources provide only short sound bites that they believe will find their way into our consciousness.

To rely only on quick sound bites that we hear throughout the day from radio, print, and TV media, internet sources, social media, and everyday human interaction is not the way to form opinions that guide our life decisions. Unfortunately, and most concerning is that all too often, we do!

Those who present news and refer to themselves as journalists should be presenting news to inform, not opinions to influence, right? Well, sometimes.

For example, in 2016, we saw examples where one major evening news anchor (NBC) was suspended and then permanently replaced for not reporting factually and embellishing his personal experiences relating to news accounts. And second, where a Sunday morning news anchor (ABC), referred to as a network's chief political journalist, apologized for his lack of transparency regarding donations to past and present political figures he had once worked for.

These are supposedly trusted national news journalists, or are they? Remember the question: Are these so-called journalists more interested in personal ambitions and agendas, or are they truly concerned with factual, unbiased news accounts? Please ask yourselves this and carefully evaluate your conclusion.

I believe we should have our eyes wide open and demand that that those who present the news do so in a factual, fair, and balanced manner.

What would be the result if a news organization purposely held back certain known facts from an important news story?

Would this be an example of silent thought? Yes, most definitely. So, you can see how easily this could be the case. Think about how damaging and counterproductive this intentional action can be if done by our major news outlets.

We should accept the fact that many and I mean many, in our major news outlets, both in television and print, decided to construct their news accounts in the most negative view possible, simply to discredit former President Trump throughout his entire term, and continues today in his post presidency. They also present false narratives of the crises that truly face America!

Now consider these same major new outlets and how they are reporting on President Biden's actions and his administration. Please be objective as you compare their reporting as it relates to these two Presidents.

Also, consider how these same news outlets reported on Hillary Clinton and Donald Trump throughout the 2016 presidential race.

This exercise should help you understand how biased and unbalanced our new media has become.

These so-called news journalists have put factual news to the side and choose only to report distorted and incomplete news in an overtly biased manner.

This could not be more destructive for America as we work our way through this current transition.

I believe that many people mistake opinions for factual news, which can easily happen if so-called unbiased news reports are really rooted in the opinions of the presenter.

Remember, we are discussing this in the context of spontaneous thought. How do we combat this and not repeat these sound bites to others we encounter, perpetuating misinformation and furthering a false narrative?

In fairness, depending on the topic, this may not be concerning. But if this is a topic with significant importance to the American way of life, our lives, and those closest to us, we must rethink our approach to this tendency and find ways to counteract it.

Should we be more discerning when we choose our news outlets? Yes, without question!

Should we choose to hear different views on major topics to better inform ourselves before choosing a position? Yes, most definitely!

One of my greatest concerns is that with the many challenges in our daily lives, we sometimes block out the most important issues affecting our way of life. If we rely only on spontaneous thought, we could be yielding the freedoms that allow us to choose independent thought and expression.

As an example, ask yourself, are we more concerned with a news story about Bruce Jenner becoming Caitlin Jenner than politics on the local and national level that have dramatic effects on the American way of life?

Unfortunately, in many cases we focus more on the notoriety of a Jenner story than politics.

Let's think about the print media, such as our major city newspapers. Ask yourself why you read a newspaper. Is it for national news, sports, finance, the local sports and news, or just the lighter side pages, such as travel and trends or the comics? Perhaps you are more interested in the editorial and op-ed pages.

Have you ever heard the phrase *above and below the fold*, which intends to highlight the major news story or stories of the day? In most cases, front-page stories present an introduction to a story of varying length, followed by a notation to find the remaining story on a page within the newspaper. Also, closely evaluate the story "headline" and evaluate the wording and whether it is biased or just factual.

Is this done for a particular reason? Is it possible that the paper wants you to page through additional pages, possibly stopping as other story lines or advertisements that catch your attention? Yes and no.

By the way, when reading my Sunday paper, I do page through, and there it is every week, that same Rolex watch ad, and I think, *well, maybe someday*, and then continue to the next page.

I do not have an issue with this practice or any other to market a product. The print media has faced a great deal of competition with the onset of the internet, and you will find many people reading tablets or other handheld devices instead of a traditional newspaper.

Why choose a newspaper when you already have access to the internet and in most cases would have to purchase the newspaper? Possibly we prefer newspapers because we do not want to surf the net, and a particular paper has the diversity to satisfy our need for information or creates a different comfort level.

However, what I do have a problem with is this: if within these so-called major news stories, the writer tries to construct the story in a way to influence the reader with personal agendas rather than simply stating the factual account of the story. If true, ask yourself, should this paper not confine these opinions to its editorial page or op-ed pages?

But let's get back to the spontaneous thought. How does what I just described affect our thought process? Certainly, when we decide to pick up a newspaper or magazine, we intend to spend more time on thought than just casual interaction. Here, spontaneous thought occurs if we read a news account of importance and form an opinion without applying any validation of the story's accuracy.

Remember the point about a newspaper's front page and whether we simply accept the headline and the first few sentences of the story as accurate, never reading the balance of the story in a later page. Those who construct these headlines do so in a way to capture our attention quickly, and if they are only trying to influence our thought rather than truly report unbiased accounts, they have taken advantage of our tendency to accept this spontaneous thought as truthful.

This is also a strategy to take advantage of our tendency to react with impulse, in the same way we sometimes react to advertisements and quickly purchase an item without any real thought or possible consequences. If we only act impulsively, those in the news media with questionable and biased agendas have accomplished their goals very quickly.

So, this is very much an example of silent thought, meaning we do not take the time to apply additional thought to validate accuracy. Please bear in mind that I am not suggesting that we painstakingly take these steps with every topic and thought we encounter. As I described earlier, we have many thoughts that are not significant. I am speaking of the major aspects of our lives and how the actions of others can have a great effect on our way of life.

I strongly encourage spontaneous thought; think of all the great improvements to our quality of life that would not exist if thoughts were not articulated or acted on, resulting in a wide variety of positive changes in our daily lives.

Many of these certainly started as a spontaneous thought and, if not acted upon, would have fallen into the silent thought chamber of our brain, possibly never to be heard of again.

Conversely, examine how incorrect thought has had adverse effects on human lives. Remember, one of my reasons for writing this book is rooted in my determination to understand what promotes thought or the lack of thought altogether, and then understand why thought does not progress to expression in either word or action.

I would also like to emphasize that we can relate spontaneous and silent thought to all aspects of our lives. However, I am greatly concerned with how our American political system exploits silent thought and will concentrate on that concept.

Silent thought can be found in everyone, irrespective of who you are, employed or unemployed, at all income levels, those highly educated and those less educated. There will be varying degrees of silent thought due to these factors.

Ask yourself, do I really need to spend my valuable time or even my idle time thinking about politics? Does politics, national and local, really affect every aspect of my life? Yes, to both, without question. Both directly and indirectly.

With greater awareness, we can proceed to look at what we should do about it. If we never experience thought on national or more global issues, we may be yielding our right to participate in the future of our country. Worst of all, we may be allowing those in politics and those in the media who promote their own agendas to influence our thoughts and only follow their direction.

Would this be an example of identity theft? Yes, ours! Please think about this and honestly evaluate the validity of your thought. You may be very surprised at the results.

CHAPTER 2

Targeted Thought

Targeted thought can happen in two primary ways, either initiated by us or by others!

First, it happens when we take the initiative to choose a topic and study it, usually with some degree of research. Hopefully, this is a subject of importance (it usually is), but what prompts this action?

Is it due to personal decisions needed or workplace decisions that require our focus? Yes, to both. Each and every day, we are constantly changing our thought priorities as we develop from infancy through adulthood. So, along this path, our targeted thoughts will change.

Let's think more in terms of our targeted thought relating to personal decisions. I think of these in two categories: first, those that govern our values, moral consciousness, and character, and then second, those that we choose for entertainment, which can be found in so many ways.

I do not believe it is necessary for us to cover workplace decisions here, as there are so many. However, I will stress that in our workplace decisions, we should still apply targeted thought with respect to how those decisions can affect the other aspects of our daily lives. Please do not leave any thoughts relating to work in that silent thought chamber of your brain.

Now, with respect to targeted thought on personal decisions, let's concern ourselves with the first category mentioned above that develops and governs our values, moral consciousness, and character. For now, let's leave to the side the second category relating to our choices for entertainment.

What do you attribute your personal development to? What and who has influenced your beliefs?

Have you emulated a person or persons in your family or a circle of friends, or have you chosen a figure by name and stature to emulate?

How much time do you spend thinking about these traits and values?

What is in your personal toolkit; strengths, weaknesses, achievements, successes, failures?

These are all very good questions to ask and not just once in a lifetime. We should challenge ourselves to assess our character traits, values, and morality as many times as necessary throughout our lives.

Once you do this, it is extremely important to find balance in the flow of information you allow to enter the brain. Don't allow just one source to dictate or trigger thought and your analysis. We should be objective and open-minded when forming our character and beliefs.

Let's hope that our foundations are strong, meaning we have received a great deal of influence from our parents and those who have guided us during our childhood to adulthood, allowing us to build on a strong footing.

This is not to say that every one of us has been fortunate enough to have a guiding hand in our childhood development. Do not worry. If you are thinking about this honestly and believe in yourself, you can and will find a path to build your character.

Have you ever thought about why you are the way you are? Are you unsure about what has impacted your character traits, beliefs, and values, yet at the same time you know you possess these characteristics that cause the actions you take in life?

This may be a result of silent thought—meaning, over a period of time, you have subjected yourself, as we all do, to the many facets of life, opinions, and actions of others, so that now your beliefs and opinions are greatly influenced by others and are not a result of your own thoughtful analysis.

I am always amazed at how uninformed or misinformed some of us are with respect to our American political system, given the access that most Americans have to the internet.

This is a tremendous source for multiple sources of information, to guide our thought processes and not be limited or subjected to the targeted influences of others. Even if you do not have access to the internet, there is always the public library.

Today's internet search engines provide us with an incredible opportunity to quickly seek out information, along with many differing views.

Yet we do not spend any significant amount of time on our country's politics and politicians, which have a great deal of influence on our freedoms to make our personal life choices. Why? Well, part of the reason is what we discussed earlier. We just don't think it is worth our time, and we have not connected the dots in the way that would allow us to see the impact on our lives, and instead we would rather embrace the more enjoyable aspects of life.

After all, we have lives filled with many challenges and obligations, so how can we possibly take the time to worry about politics? Politicians know this and exploit this. Don't give up. There is a solution, so please keep reading!

Warning: please very mindful that some internet and social media sites can and do target your thought with distortions and are very biased, especially as it relates to our national politics.

The second primary way targeted thought can occur is when actions are initiated by other parties that specifically attempt to influence our thoughts and then influence our actions and beliefs.

Now, I do want to mention that this can be just fine and is something that many of us welcome, as we want to be presented with stimuli and enjoy our daily consumption of all sorts of information. Others are more guarded and limit the intake from unsolicited sources, deciding to search out information and clarity on topics by initiating targeted thought, as described earlier in this chapter.

Targeted thought will come at us in many ways, written and spoken via many conduits, radio, television, print sources such as newspapers and magazines, the internet, blogs, social sites, and more.

Just think of all the ways you encounter information throughout your workday; it's almost dizzying.

For example, think about all the advertisements embedded in your favorite newspaper, magazine, or website. You may be simply reading a news account or searching out an answer, and there they are, the graphics, popups, banners, or whatever, to redirect your attention to an ad.

Ask yourself, why don't these sources just place all these ads in one section? Is it because they do not want it to be your choice to check out an advertisement? Of course, it is!

We live in the greatest country in the world, with a vibrant capitalistic economy. So, we should enjoy and take advantage of free competition for all to participate in either as a seller or buyer of goods, services, and information.

Certainly, we should be discerning and objective in how we let these influences affect our actions.

Let's now think about those who intentionally target our thoughts and take initiatives to not only influence our thought but also modify our political and social beliefs.

What would the outcome be if this was done in an insidious way, with the express desire to modify our thinking and not for any other reason? Let's look closer at the meaning of the word *insidious* as *Webster's Dictionary* defines it: "awaiting a chance to entrap; treacherous, harmful but enticing, having a gradual and cumulative effect." Carefully review that definition and ask yourself, are our politicians, political pundits (those who think they know what is in the best interest for America) and those in the news media with personal ambitions and political agendas capable of engaging in this behavior?

Yes, without question!

Not every politician or those affiliated with the political process engage in this deception, but many do. It is also fair to say that not all of those in the media act this way, but again, many do.

The most disturbing part of this is that the so-called news journalists in this country should be an objective filter between those in politics and us, the American public. Additionally, these journalists must vet every politician in the same way, irrespective of party affiliation.

The next time you watch or hear a press interview with a politician or political strategist, take notice of the context of the question.

Is it a well-constructed inquiry to an important topic that would challenge the responding party to answer succinctly and honestly, or is it simply a question that only allows the responding party to respond with platitudes, vagueness, and no relevance to the question asked?

Watch different news programs and honestly compare the competence of the interviewer and the seriousness of his or her questions. Please include a source that you typically do not watch or listen to, not opinion talk shows but so-called news programs.

One revealing indicator to notice is, after the responding party does not answer the question, even though he or she just spoke for several minutes, does the interviewer restate or press for an answer to the question or just accept a non-answer and move on to the next question to be avoided?

Ask yourself, is the interviewer just making an appearance of asking a probing question with no real interest in a relevant response? Yes, in many cases.

Ask yourself, why would a so-called serious news journalist with many years of experience allow distortion of factual news in this way?

Is this not just an example of a journalist using his or her forum to further a politician's or political party's agenda, which means he or she has the same agenda? Sure it is!

Is this news? Of course not. It is a deliberate attempt to target our thought process with agendas to alter our beliefs. They disguise this process as news and not opinion, because if they did identify it as opinion and not news, very few of us would accept them as credible unbiased news outlets.

Some of us will quickly see this and will discredit it. Unfortunately, many of us accept this encounter as factual news and repeat the falsehood many times. Again, silent thought occurs.

We should not allow spontaneous and targeted thought to misguide us, which is what they are hoping for.

The press should not act as a conduit between a politician or political party and the American public by taking a politician's or party's agenda and reporting that as factual news. They should not pick and choose in this way. If they do, we should immediately remove them from our chosen news sources.

If we want opinion, we can easily find that, but when it comes to presenting the critical news accounts of the day, we must demand facts, and only the facts. It is a waste of our valuable time to do otherwise, and we should accept nothing less.

Believe me, once these institutions and those who practice this realize that we now understand these tactics, they will change or become irrelevant.

Remember this: those who engage in this malpractice have refined this greatly and disguise their behavior very well. They will also take the long view, the same way for example that advertisers do, meaning they will constantly target your thought process to eventually convince you to adopt their beliefs and values.

This may be okay when deciding to buy a car or home or undertaking the many other life choices. But choosing whom to vote for or taking a misinformed position based on tainted facts can lead to a serious erosion of every freedom we cherish.

Remember my earlier comment about identity theft and impulsive behavior. So, you can see they rely on two primary tactics to alter our beliefs. Please do not let this happen to you!

I do want to mention that television and radio opinion talk shows of a political nature can be very valuable. Why? Hearing different points of view is an important step in keeping an open mind.

Listening to nationally syndicated radio shows who allow their listeners to call in and express their concerns is also very helpful in truly understanding all of America's thoughts and concerns.

They also can stimulate our thinking in different ways, depending on who is engaging in the debate. It can help you to allow the subject of politics to take up more of your consciousness.

I encourage you not to simply listen to shows that only have hosts and guests of the same opinion; this is boring and counterproductive. Choose programs that offer point and counterpoint formats and that have guests with different political opinions and beliefs. You will find this much more stimulating to your thought process.

Those who offer only one belief and ridicule those with differing views don't want intellectual debates, and you will find these are the same people trying to target your thoughts, which is okay, as long as you realize this is happening.

If you decide to listen to an opinion talk show, you expect to hear opinions, which everyone is entitled to and is a true expression of our freedoms.

Without question, the COVID-19 pandemic, and the presidential election, were two major drivers of targeted thought in 2020. Please consider all the distortion and falsehoods that we were subjected to by our media and our state and federal representatives, which continued throughout 2021.

One further point on these so-called news journalists. In many cases they may or may not be biased, but they are simply not prepared or informed enough about their question. So, during an interview, they are not able to push back after their guest responds with falsehoods or distractions.

Then in other news programs we see too much equivocation in their reporting on national politics, meaning they try to apply both sides of the story to appear more balanced. This in many cases only confuses an important issue. Facts are facts and they should be prepared enough to confidently state a news story irrespective of whether or not it casts a negative light on a particular political party.

Again, these formats are simply a waste of our valuable time and further pushes these serious issues from America's consciousness!

In the last two chapters, we have discussed both spontaneous and targeted thought, along with how and why silent thought occurs.

In the next chapter, we will discuss stubborn thought, which is important to consider as in many instances is a result of how we process spontaneous and targeted thought.

In the following chapters, I hope to further explain how politics is interwoven into every American's life. We will discuss our current state of transition and several crises currently facing America.

I hope my readers gain a better understanding of when and how silent thought interconnects with these major crises of our day.

In the final chapter, we will discuss how all the crises are inter-connected, and we will further discuss solutions to combat silent thought.

CHAPTER 3

Stubborn Thought

You may be asking, why am I considering the concept of stubborn thought in this book? Good question.

As I noted in closing chapter two, stubborn thought often forms because of the negative impacts of spontaneous and targeted thought. This can be problematic if we are more prone to stubbornness in our approach to life. *Webster's Dictionary* defines *stubborn* as "unreasonably obstinate, hard or stiff, difficult to shape or work." It also defines it as "fixed or set in purpose or opinion, resolute."

When you consider these definitions, you can see both positive and negative aspects. Certainly, being purposed and resolute can be a valuable trait in many aspects of our daily lives.

However, being unreasonably obstinate or difficult to work or interact with can be an impediment in managing our daily lives. It can also be challenging if our opinions are fixed and incapable of considering alternative viewpoints.

Ask yourself, are you a stubborn person in the context of the definition I noted above and please be honest. I know from my personal life experiences, I have exhibited varying degrees of stubborn behavior with both positive and often negative consequences.

Also ask yourself, if those close to you in both family and work settings would describe you as stubborn. I would like to think that this exercise is a very worthwhile conversation we should all have with ourselves.

But let's get back to stubborn thought. If we refuse to consider alternate viewpoints simply because we have locked in a personal belief, is this not an example of stubborn thought? This is also when silent thought kicks in, meaning we just simply refuse to give any critical thought to a particular issue or discussion.

Think of the potential loss of valuable insight and knowledge when we allow stubborn thought to overtake our thought analysis! This is especially true if we have formed our opinions because of spontaneous or targeted thought as I have explained in earlier chapters.

Critical thought analysis does not have to govern our entire day. Many of us do apply more critical thought to the things closest to our individual lives. However, as we qualify what we believe is less important to our daily lives, we push it further and further from our critical thought analysis.

So, if we tend to be more stubborn, we may shrink even further the amount of time we think about the many important issues facing our country.

One very important crisis facing our country is our political process, especially at the national level. This is not so much an issue at the local level simply because it is the closest to the communities where we live and work and we tend to give it more thought and, in some cases, get personally involved.

But as we move further from local politics to state and most certainly our national politics, many of us never really apply any critical thought. This is where I really believe stubborn thought overtakes any willingness to consider an alternate political perspective.

Think back to the last time you had a discussion with someone regarding national politics or, more specifically, a national political figure. How long into that discussion did it take before you stopped considering or simply just stopped listening and silently dismissed everything the other person was saying?

Now this may be appropriate if we really believe that we have previously applied critical thought analysis to the subject being discussed. However, if we simply stop listening and shut down our brain's ability to discern and consider other viewpoints, is this not another example of silent thought and mindless encounters? Sure, it is!

Please resist this tendency, especially when the subject of national politics and policy arise. Those politicians who target our thoughts with only their personal agendas in mind prefer an America divided, once they have accomplished their goal of forming our political thought for us.

In the subtitle of this book, *America in Transition and Crisis*, the word "transition" speaks to the importance of choice and direction.

When we consider the important choices facing our nation, how could we possibly choose the right direction without considering all viewpoints in an intellectually honest and unbiased manner?

Well, the answer is simple, we will not be able to move forward as a unified nation!

A serious and destructive consequence of stubborn thought, as it relates to politics, is the tendency to become angry or literally develop hatred of others who simply disagree with your political position.

The number of Americans who have reacted with nothing but disdain for President Trump and his election is alarming. Families and friends have ended relationships due to their different opinions on President Trump.

The anti-Trump media is responsible in large part for this division with their deceptive and divisive reporting of Trump's positions and initiatives!

We are now in a post Trump presidency and see a new Biden presidency and a national media trying to completely erase the Trump era. This is not unifying, only divisive.

We all must resist the undue influences of others who prefer division and hatred in their pursuit to reshape America with indifference to our constitution and founding principles!

As we move through the next five chapters, I will spend more time on President Obama's two terms than the other presidents mentioned, as I believe his actions and policies did dramatically worsen the crises I discuss in this book.

Stubborn thought is on full display in today's America with respect to our politicians and the path forward.

So, as we close this chapter, please resist stubbornness to open thought and expression, but please be very stubborn in our need to change the politics in Washington, DC, in a positive way that will endure for generations to come.

A closed mind has only one path—failure. Conversely, an open mind will easily find the path to lasting success and American greatness!

CHAPTER 4

American Crisis Number One— Leadership in America

Whom do you look to for leadership? Many people might say God, parents, a sibling, a teacher, or a coach.

How many times have we changed our minds about whom we choose as a leader? How many times have we been disappointed in our leaders? I would like to think that we will change as many times as necessary, but ask yourself, what makes an effective leader?

Have you ever noticed that those who proclaim to be a leader are not really leading but are trying to advocate a personal belief that may or may not be in the best interest of the people that follow him or her?

Have you ever thought about the *perception principle*? This principle identifies three views: first, how you perceive yourself; second, how you think others perceive you; and third, how others actually do perceive you.

The answers could be very different among all three, and the third might really surprise many of us.

If we do not lead, then what is our role? Are we simply just followers? Yes, there are many of us who just follow the lead of others. Certainly, there are many of us who are leaders with respect to our own lives and those of our children. But outside of the family unit, are we taking any leadership roles?

Sure we do, in all walks of life, both in our workplaces and in our places of worship. I would like to point out—some may agree and others not—that the exception to those leaders that might fail us is God, who is infallible This book is not written from this perspective, but it is an important distinction to mention. However, and very concerning, is that we continue see a sustained push to remove God from our daily lives.

I would like to see America become a nation of leaders, with all its citizens in leadership roles, taking responsibility for their own lives and holding those in politics accountable for their actions. Have you ever heard the saying "take an ownership mentality"? Think about it. Unfortunately, many citizens allow silent thought to restrict their ability to lead in this way. Our strength as a nation resides in our citizens, not in a few politicians in Washington, DC. So please do not ever yield your leadership role!

Now, let's think about leadership in more depth regarding our politicians, both in local and national offices. Politicians often forget that we elect them to take the lead on issues and follow a direction we believe to be in our best interest, not try to lead us in a direction of policy that they believe is in our best interest.

This is one of the reasons we are so disappointed in many of our so-called political leaders. This is also why we must focus and think more about this crisis at this time.

I am going to focus the rest of this chapter on leaders that hold national office rather than try to look at local politicians. However, the same deficiencies exist at your local level as well.

Considering the focus of this book, let's look at the top six leaders in our government: the president, vice president, speaker of the house, senate majority leader, house minority leader, and senate minority leader.

First, our president. I will cite several elections, between 2000 and 2020. Let's start with 2008.

In the 2008 Democrat presidential primary, I enthusiastically supported Barack Obama. I did so for two very important reasons in my view.

His chief rival was Hillary Clinton, who in my analysis was not the right choice for our nation. I felt it would be more politics as usual, the same old lip service, and I was uncomfortable with many of her core beliefs.

Additionally, I just did not find her trustworthy and felt her to be too partisan. Too many instances of her embellishing her life experiences, too much of a politician. I simply did not see her as an inclusive leader and possessing true leadership qualities.

Mrs. Clinton again entered the race for the Democrat nomination, this time in the 2016, and did become her party's nominee. My concerns from 2008 had only grown stronger when considering her candidacy. Further thoughts on this in a later chapter.

Now my first reason for supporting Mr. Obama. I felt he presented a reasonable possibility for change for the better in our broken political system—that simple. I was optimistic that he could accomplish his stated goals for change in American politics.

Sure, I listened very closely to all the arguments against his candidacy—inexperience, too new to national politics, and many more, but felt he could overcome these challenges if he would truly put the interest of all Americans over those entrenched political interests in Washington, DC. I did consider the Republican primary candidates but felt they represented just more of the same failed political deception.

As the primary season ended and as we moved through the general election, I was delighted to see the country's excitement level continue to rise at the prospect of Obama winning the presidency.

I believe this was for many reasons, including the prospect that our country would see positive change in how our government conducted itself and the enthusiasm that change was possible, and certainly, not the least of reasons was that America would elect its first black president.

After the election, I felt it important to monitor President Obama's actions and words. For the first several months, I watched and listened to the daily White House press briefings and whatever presidential orders, or statements were issued, as well as the president's approach to naming his cabinet.

I found that whitehouse.gov and CSPAN were very helpful in providing access to these daily events. Doing this was challenging, due to all my other commitments, but I felt this necessary to determine whether my thought process was correct in voting for Mr. Obama.

I was also very anxious to see tangible change and if campaign promises were kept or if they just found their way out the president's consciousness.

As this president's first year in office progressed, I started to notice a more rigid ideology take hold. Having strong core beliefs is certainly part of effective leadership, but rigid ideology without the willingness for debate is counterproductive and not in America's best interest.

During his first two years in office, President Obama's party controlled both the US House of Representatives and the US Senate. The speaker of the house was Nancy Pelosi, and the senate majority leader was Harry Reid. These two individuals also demonstrated strong tendencies toward rigid ideology and were very partisan.

The narrative by many, not all, in the political sphere that started to develop was that if one were to disagree with or criticize President Obama, his or her motive, if white, must be racially motivated. Of course, this was simply ridiculous and used only as a distraction instead of engaging in an honest exchange of ideas and debate on the issue in question. This was just the beginning of a period of the most destructive type of divisive politics that consumed Washington, DC, and our country during Obama's two terms.

The reason for mentioning this is that we can see how silent thought is employed by those who wish to distract and shut down debate.

The racial nature of this narrative created silent thought among many Americans, who decided not to participate in any discussion with dissenting views, for fear of being labeled a racist.

Is any of this leadership? Of course not!

Presidential leadership is rooted in the office of the president, not in the person holding that office. The person coming into the office brings leadership qualities that either enhance the presidency or diminish it.

A key quality that must exist in presidential leadership is the ability to inspire greatness in each and every citizen, not just the ones that support your views and cast their ballot in your favor.

The presidency is not about the greatness of one man or one woman; it is the greatness of America as a unified, thriving nation that leads the world in every aspect of human achievement.

So why would any politician practice politics to divide rather than to unite? Well, unfortunately the answer is that they are pursuing personal ambitions rather than American greatness.

Do you remember our discussion in a prior chapter regarding insidious motives? Ask yourself, does this behavior meet that definition?

Sadly, I believe that President Obama was practicing divisive politics, meaning he saw the need to divide America along the lines of race, gender, age, wealth, and political ideology.

In doing this, he distracted many from the vital need to solve the serious challenges we face as a nation. This is not what he promised during his campaign!

He is not the only politician to practice this. Many, irrespective of party affiliation, have practiced these same destructive tactics, as well as many in the media and many inside of our political institutions.

I know some of my readers will push back on this assertion, and I respect that. I ask you to fairly evaluate the eight years of the Obama presidency.

Please do not rely on all the targeted sound bites you have heard during his presidency and post-presidency that have secured their place in your consciousness. Rather, resist the silent thought tendency and challenge yourself to truly evaluate his leadership.

Please ask yourself the following:

- Was President Obama more concerned with personal ambition and legacy than anything else?
- Did he spend more time applauding America's greatness or more time apologizing for or criticizing America?
- Did he project humility in the office he held, or did he project arrogance and a sense of being more important than that same office?
- Did he completely politicize every major issue facing our nation?

Please search out the answers to these questions with your critical thought and analysis and not by just accepting the opinions of others.

I am not comfortable in criticizing our president, past or present, because of the great respect that I have for the office of the presidency and our country, but I feel it vital that we insist that the person who holds the presidency be held accountable and truly be an inspirational leader for all Americans.

Another very important leadership quality to have as president is the ability to ensure those you appoint to major cabinet posts are delivering their respective agency services fairly and then to hold them accountable when they don't perform their responsibilities in the best interest of the American people.

It is important to note that these appointments should not be a way to reward big donors or partisans. But rather to appoint those well qualified with respect to the cabinet or agency in question. Any other consideration is not in the best interest for our nation.

Let's look at two agencies during the Obama years. The first is the IRS. This agency not only spent millions of dollars on wasteful, so-called work-related seminars or retreats that were laughable and unnecessary but was also allowed to target tax-exempt groups for their political beliefs to restrict their views and freedoms.

The second example is the Veterans Administration hospitals across this country, where it was discovered that our vets were waiting months for care, received inadequate care or no care at all, and in many cases were treated as faceless numbers rather than the heroes they are.

Some of our vets that survived the battlefield tragically lost their lives while waiting for the proper care they so justly deserved from these VA hospitals!

This VA hospital example is still a serious problem at the time of writing this book but did improve under President Trump through needed legislation along with leadership and policy changes. Search out the number of our vets committing suicide each day. You will be shocked!

When President Obama was asked when he was made aware of these issues, his response was that he heard about them like every other American, through news accounts. From that day forward until his final day in office, very little was done to correct this. You see, this was an inconvenient truth that Obama and many in the news media simply ignored.

Ask yourself, being completely honest in your thought process, is this leadership? Absolutely not!

Also, look at the distractions presented by the media and others in trying to deflect blame regarding these two examples. This is another display of how targeted thought is used to manipulate our thoughts through meaningless sound bites in the hope that the American public will accept the excuses and move on.

Please do not ever accept the excuse from any politician or any defender of the status quo that a government agency is very complicated, and therefore solutions are difficult, and the American public must be more patient or more understanding.

This could not be further from the truth. One of the reasons these breakdowns (some refer to as scandals) in government occur is because government is too large, which creates an unaccountable bureaucracy and workforce.

It was truly disheartening to see President Obama act in this way. I had very high expectations for him when he took office. Could he have made a course correction?

To change, he would have had to accept the fact that the office he held was not about him or his legacy but rather the future of the American people, and he was there to safeguard that future, not further his own political and personal ambitions!

Unfortunately, I do not think he has the humility or the capacity to think of it in this way and was consumed with his rigid ideology. He has his own opinions, and we should respect that. However, he was gravely wrong—no bias, just strong disagreement.

I can respect his policy views, but I cannot agree with the tactic of divisive politics, which only accomplishes further division and strife in our country.

Let's look at two former presidents, John Kennedy and Ronald Reagan, and two quotes from each—first from John Kennedy: "Ask not what your country can do for you, ask what you can do for your country"; and second from Ronald Reagan: "Peace through strength." These comments were made in similar contexts and were made more than twenty years apart.

These two presidents had great leadership qualities and understood that the greatness of America and a united citizenry are far more important than a single person occupying the White House.

Without question, these two former presidents had flaws, as we all do under God, but did lead with America's interest in the forefront.

One of the most important responsibilities of the presidency is to protect our nation from all foreign enemies that seek to destroy America and those that wish to kill Americans either here or around the world.

Many have said, and I strongly agree, "That those who seek to harm America should so fear us that they would never want to meet us on the battlefield, but rather instead choose to sit across from us at the negotiating table."

The way we accomplish this and ensure the freedoms that we cherish is to have a military second to none. Our military should be stronger than that of any other two or three countries' militaries combined that are closest to our military's capacity and who currently threaten the world.

I know that some will challenge this, but those who do, ignore not only world history but American history and how America has defeated evil time and time again.

I will however, stress that our military needs reform, not reduction!

It must possess the highest levels of technology, tactical weaponry, and strategic dominance along with the best and brightest personnel. So, when I say stronger, I don't mean just simply more personnel.

The reform I am speaking about is dealing with the wasteful spending that has crept into our military structure, as it has in many of our other government agencies. Our military budget requires a large percentage of our tax dollars, and the military must be held accountable for every dollar it spends.

This is where others are wrong, thinking that just cutting our military budget or the number of personnel is the answer. And yes, our politicians politicize our military, and that must stop!

Our military's leaders, along with its civilian counterparts, must always look several years ahead and plan accordingly. How in the world did we ever allow ISIS to reach its deadly prominence?

Who failed America here? Our president or our military?

President Obama did not understand or chose not to accept the reality of what a country's military provides its citizens.

Our nation cannot continue to thrive without the assurances of a military that ensures our protection and our ability to practice the liberty and freedoms that have created America's greatness, which is the envy of the world!

President Obama chose to reduce our military and, in his efforts, to marginalize the United States as just another nation in a world of many, and to diminish our standing as a superpower.

This could not be more dangerous to America and the world! JFK and Ronald Reagan understood the importance of our military's strength and how and when to use it.

The US president is often referred to as the leader of the free world by many around the world. The key word here is *leader*. If this person is not an effective leader, the consequences can be disastrous not only for America but for the entire free world.

I ask you; did President Obama behave as the leader of the free world?

Here again, it is important to remember that the person holding the office of president is not the force that the world is looking to but rather a united America as the force for leadership in the world.

Therefore, if our president projects strength, then America will appear strong, and conversely, if our president projects weakness, America will appear weak and will be challenged over and over again, both militarily and strategically.

President Obama's negotiation with Iran over their ambitions to develop and deliver a nuclear weapon was one of the most vivid examples of his weakness as a leader.

Why do I say this? Well, let's consider some very important aspects.

When entering these negotiations, America possessed a very powerful position. Unified sanctions with other nations against Iran were in place, which is really what brought Iran to the negotiating table in the first place—Iran's economy in turmoil, along with fear of military strikes by Israel or the United States.

So, what did President Obama and the then secretary of state John Kerry, another weak leader, do? They yielded to Iran's demands and, by doing so, weakened our position of strength.

They also agreed to more and more extensions to find a way to make a deal. Why would they do this?

Instead of showing weakness by granting extensions, why did they not just suspend negotiations?

Why did Obama not let Iran see that he might agree with congress and toughen the sanctions?

Did they not enter these talks with a clear vision of what was at stake and what would be the nonnegotiable concessions that Iran would have to make?

Why would he act as if we were negotiating a deal with a friendly country or ally rather than dealing with the seriousness of an enemy trying to develop a nuclear weapon and a country that would likely use it or allow one of its proxies to use it?

Were we not adept enough to understand Iran for who they really are, a state sponsor of terrorism and a country where its leader and people continually shout, "Death to America and Israel"?

Has Iran not participated in or been a party to the death of American soldiers in Iraq and elsewhere?

Do we not believe that Iran seeks to establish its dominance in the region, as other nations in that region, including Israel, have warned about many times over?

Please do not be fooled or misguided by those that were trying to make this terrible deal or those who supported it, when they were questioned about how this was being handled and responded that these negotiations were very delicate and complicated, and the American people needed to be patient. Really!

There was nothing complicated about these negotiations!

Sure, some diplomatic negotiations between nations can be very difficult and require concessions on both sides. This was not one.

However, those on our side of the table were making it more complicated and very doubtful for an acceptable American result when they continually extended deadlines, yielded to Iran's demands, and treated this as if they were negotiating with a trustworthy nation.

We had all the leverage yet were behaving in a timid and weak manner, as if Iran held leverage over us and its neighbors.

How incompetent was it of Obama and Kerry not to recognize this? Ask yourself, why were we even discussing lifting sanctions until Iran signed an unconditional agreement to stop and dismantle its nuclear program?

Then they must demonstrate that they are adhering to the agreement, including unchallenged inspections. Then and only then should we start to phase in any relief in sanctions.

One of the reasons Russia and China wanted an agreement and the arms embargo lifted was so that they could sell weapons and weapon systems to Iran.

Did this stabilize this region or further destabilize the region? Is the answer not obvious?

Did anyone really believe that it would be easy to snap back the sanctions, as President Obama insisted, if Iran failed to honor the agreement? The naive behavior of those negotiating for America was stunning.

The other tactic they employed was to use a straw man argument, such as if we did not find a deal, then what is the other alternative? War?

You see, when they use the word *war*, they intend to frighten Americans over that prospect and silence those who disagree.

They were attempting to remove the American citizen from the decision process and convince us that we could not possibly understand this diplomatic effort or label those who disagree as warmongers.

Americans are much smarter than to be fooled by these distractions or illusions and must not allow those who are disingenuous on this subject to target our thoughts in this way.

President Obama sought his way and only his way by distorting the facts when speaking to the American public.

Some have said the reason for all this illogical behavior by Obama and Kerry was desperation for any deal to enhance their respective legacies.

This was simply another example of Obama politicizing a critical issue, one of national security, rather taking a straightforward America-first approach?

It was very concerning to see America embarrassed by their incompetence, which only gave Iran and the rest of the world the impression that a signed deal was more important than all the perils of Iran securing a nuclear weapon and the means to deliver it with an intercontinental ballistic missile.

After the deal was agreed to, what did our president do?

He sent the agreement to the United Nations Security Council to be voted on before even sending it to congress so that America, through its elected representatives, could have an opportunity to review and either vote to approve or disapprove.

Why would President Obama not put America first instead of looking to the UN first?

Well first, again on display was his arrogance, where he thinks his view should be accepted without question. Second, he believed that UN approval would give this deal more influence over the US Congress.

Again, he was trying to manipulate America's thought through the appearance that it must be a good deal if the UN approved of it.

Ask yourself, why did we not insist on the four Americans being held by Iran at the time, to be released as part of this agreement?

President Obama and Secretary Kerry both made conflicting comments on why this was not considered or accomplished. Not ensuring their release further highlighted to the world the incompetence and weakness of these leaders and their failure to negotiate from a position of strength.

This was made part of the conversation only after President Obama was embarrassed by a question during a press conference.

Then after the nuclear deal was finalized, we find that at the same time the hostages were released, President Obama authorized a $400-million-dollar payment to Iran. When discovered, his response was that this not ransom but rather the first payment of the $1.7 billion agreed to in settlement with Iran over a dispute on a military arms deal after the uprising in 1979.

Ask yourself the following:

- Why was this payment made at the very same time as the hostages were set to be released?
- Why was this payment made in cash in foreign currencies?
- Why did this president have to admit that they did prevent any access to this payment by Iran until the held Americans were airborne?

Obama and those in his administration applauded their actions in reaching a deal at The Hague Tribunal that was formed to deal with the disputes between the US and Iran that they settled rather than taking the risk that this tribunal might award billions more to Iran.

Why did this president feel the need to resolve this matter when other presidents before him did not? Why was he so willing to appease Iran, considering their actions against America, especially their role in deaths of so many American military men and women? Obama's willingness to deal with Iran in these ways not only embarrasses our country but simply rewarded these sponsors of terrorism with billions of dollars and cleared the path for their ability to acquire a deliverable nuclear weapon.

There must be a full accounting of these issues regarding Iran, and most importantly, we must revisit this deal on their nuclear ambitions, which was undertaken during the Trump presidency.

Did President Obama have secret communications with Iran when he first took office? Also, consider why Obama was so quiet during the 2009 Iranian uprising and deadly protests.

Before commencing any negotiations with Iran, the preconditions at the very least should have been the release of American hostages, retractions by Iran's leaders of "death to America," and Iran's leaders acknowledging the right of Israel to exist as a nation!

These are not complicated concepts, but our leaders at that time chose to serve their personal ambitions rather than serve the American people.

At no other time were the countries in the Middle East, including Saudi Arabia, Egypt, Jordan, and Turkey, as well as Israel, readier to form a coalition against Iran, waiting for America to take the lead. So, what did President Obama do? He hesitated, led from behind, ignored some of these country's leaders, and allowed more and more destabilization to occur in the region, along with deadly consequences.

Look back to the mid-1990's when President Bill Clinton gave billions to North Korea to persuade them to stop their path toward the development of nuclear weapons. When Clinton spoke to the American people, he claimed that this is a great agreement for the US and North Korea's neighbors.

While he and his sycophants were patting themselves on the back, North Korean leaders were laughing at America and already on their way to a nuclear bomb, now with US dollars to support their nuclear ambitions.

Clinton's appeasement was nothing more than a political ploy and naive understanding America's enemies.

In 2006, under George W. Bush as president, North Korea tested its first nuclear device, which went unchallenged in any meaningful way.

Now you would think with this historical account on how evil dictatorships behave, Obama would be more practical and determined when dealing with Iran's nuclear ambitions. Sadly, he demonstrated the same weak leadership as Clinton and Bush. Make no mistake about it, North Korea was not silent during Obama's two terms, as it continued to test nuclear detonations and conducted many missile test firings.

Consider Obama's approach when dealing with ISIS. Do you remember his statement that ISIS was just a JV team and did not present any threat to America? He continued this pretense until it became so serious that he was forced to change his position. His hesitation only allowed ISIS to strengthen its dominance, seize land in Iraq and Syria, and pursue its deadly activities.

Our foreign policy under President Obama faltered repeatedly and lacked any strategic thought for America's interests.

Please consider Russia, China, and North Korea as well as those in the Middle East. Are these countries creating more or less stability in the world?

When dealing with these countries, President Obama only concerned himself with a personal agenda and attempted to construct his legacy at the peril of America and the free world.

Intentionally or not, Obama's actions greatly diminished America's role as the world's only superpower!

I want to be clear. I do not have any issue with a president that is concerned with his or her legacy while in office, especially when considering the high office of the presidency and the oath of office he or she takes.

What Obama and others that have held this office fail to realize is that a president that governs with only the American people's best interests in mind—not with his or her own personal interests and ambitions shaping their decisions—will have no problem with legacy and will rank very high in our presidential history.

So again, ask yourself, being impartial, is this the type of leadership we should accept?

Would JFK or Ronald Reagan have led in this way?

I would like to cite another example of the lack of President Obama's leadership, and then we must move on to President Trump.

President Obama's continued resistance throughout his tenure to approve the Keystone Pipeline and open government land for lease for oil and natural gas exploration only further weakened our nation.

Think about all the years that we have been told by our political leaders that we need to engage the Middle East due to our dependence on oil and how that region's politics affect our nation and our foreign policy decisions.

Now, our nation, through its technology advances, has created an energy boom in natural gas and oil production. We are becoming the world's leader in oil production and currently lead in natural gas production.

Look at the benefits for America as a result—very low and sustainable gas prices, which has created more disposable income for every American, not to mention how lower energy costs have had positive benefits for other sectors of our economy, which enables growth and prosperity.

Our nation's oil production has also helped to lower oil prices on the world market, which also creates financial stress on some exporting countries that don't share our same values and worldviews, due to the high cost of extracting their oil.

Sure, American companies are experiencing the same issue, but with our technology and innovation, they will continue to reduce their cost of extraction and rise above these challenges. That's America!

So why did Obama resist this incredible opportunity for energy independence? Was he again politically motivated and simply conceding to his political base, or was it again his rigid ideology that prevented him from taking proactive steps to embrace this American opportunity?

Yes, to both questions!

Think about the benefits that having the world's strongest military along with being the world's energy leader could afford to all Americans. Not even considering a stronger economy, these are both national security imperatives.

Do you remember in the campaign leading up to the 2008 and 2012 elections, where President Obama's opponents spoke to energy independence and how Mr. Obama and his supporters ridiculed these opponents over these positions?

Do you remember his recurring comments that "you cannot drill your way out this problem," and "we should get used to the reality of higher gas prices." Again, he was completely out of touch with America!

How could one president be so wrong on so many issues?

I really believe that President Obama behaved as if he was appearing in an eight-year-long episode of "the lifestyles of the rich and famous." He was only concerned with prestige, not purpose of presidential leadership!

Once elected, his narcissism and hubris were on full display and continued throughout his two terms.

He continues these same tendencies in his post-presidency. President Obama promised to fundamentally reshape America.

Unfortunately, it has become obvious his efforts have greatly contributed to the serious transition that now faces America, were not in America's best interest, and in many ways, worsened the crises I discuss in this book!

One of the most disliked aspects of President Obama was in his response to critics that felt his actions and words were antithetical to American greatness, with Obama's response that this was somehow just a nostalgic view of America's past and not relevant in today's America. Very, very disturbing!

Now, let's discuss President Trump, who was elected in 2016 over his competitor, Hillary Clinton. He won a decisive Electoral College victory, carrying keys states considered very solid in Clinton's column. I mention his Electoral College victory as this was greatly ignored by Clinton and her supporters along with much of the main-stream media.

The first reaction to their loss was to bring into question the vote totals in the "blue wall" states of Michigan and Wisconsin. This quickly faded as recounts resulted in more Trump votes in many instances. Next, they tried to somehow delegitimize Trump's victory because Clinton won the popular vote. While this was true, it has no bearing on how our presidency is won. These were only the first in a series of many distortions and distractions promoted to target our thought process and convince America that Clinton really won and Trump in some way didn't truly win.

Take a moment and do an internet search for a map of America with states broken out by county and take notice of the broad support that Trump won. Also, consider the states of California and New York, where Clinton won the most votes, and how heavily Democrat they are. You will quickly see how disingenuous this argument is and how ridiculous those that promote this really are. If our election process was based on the popular vote, do you not think that Trump would have spent the necessary time in these two heavily populated states!

Then came the next series of distractions, Russian interference, Wikileaks, and James Comey, the former FBI director, the two-year Mueller investigation and these distortions and false narratives continued through the entire Trump presidency.

These excuses by Clinton and those who supported her along with a compliant media only reinforced America's correct choice to elect Donald Trump. Clinton was a flawed candidate, with no message that resonated with America, and most importantly, a very dishonest individual who should be prosecuted for offenses while secretary of state. She would have only continued or made worse Obama's destructive policies.

While I have several concerns with President Trump and will be critical as we move on, he was an infinitely better choice for America than Mrs. Clinton.

Mr. Trump's key campaign slogan was "Make America Great Again." The problem I have with this statement is that it suggests that one person can exert sole influence over this nation. I would rather this statement be simply "Let America Be Great Again."

I am not trying to split hairs, but America has always been a great nation. What we have experienced at times is presidential incompetence limiting this country's greatness.

My concern is, as stated earlier, the greatness of this nation is not and has never been rooted in any one person or political party. It resides in the hearts and minds of every American bound together through national unity and love of country.

Unfortunately, I believe President Trump is a narcissist, not as bad as President Obama, but certainly very absorbed with himself. Also, I believe that President Trump did not possess the temperament to hold this office. These traits are incompatible with the leadership qualities necessary for a truly successful presidency.

Many believe that Trump sought the presidency out of love of country. While I do not challenge his love for this nation, I believe that Mr. Trump chose this path because his hubris convinced him that simply if he became president, it would have to be successful solely because he was Trump. Again, not a leadership quality but rather a risk for America.

Have you ever noticed during his speeches or responses to questions, how he must always embellish the quality and total success of his actions or accomplishments? He did this with current initiatives as well as future efforts yet to happen.

Not necessary and unrealistic!

He never overcame these tendencies during his term as President and certainly worsened as it became very evident that these traits are very rooted in his personality.

I would be remiss if I did not mention that President Trump was subjected to many distortions by our biased press and his opposing party throughout his term. But his personality prevented him from taking a more appropriate response strategy.

Another slogan that became popular with Trump's victory is "Drain the Swamp," which describes the corrupt nature of our political institutions and layered bureaucracy in Washington, DC. President Trump took several important steps to address this through executive actions and his cabinet appointments and they should be applauded.

But what President Trump failed to recognize is that this swamp may be drainable but unlikely due to the sheer number of excesses that are continually refilling the swamp.

Additionally, the next president or next congress can simply reverse many of Trump's initiatives and successes, which is so evident as we now see Biden's agenda and actions in an effort to completely erase Trump's presidency.

President Trump did not address the root of this dysfunction, which are the individuals who hold these national offices, including the presidency.

He did not recognize that the first step in accomplishing this is the tenure of these politicians in Washington must be limited. He did not provide leadership on this and did not use his bully pulpit to promote term limits and nothing less!

By not doing this, his actions to drain the swamp were in vain and he simply became politically motivated and part of the swamp.

One early example of him becoming politically motivated or certainly the appearance of is when he appointed Senate Majority Leader Mitch McConnell's wife as his secretary of transportation. Qualifications aside, this is simply the same political cronyism that is pervasive throughout Washington, DC. More on this cabinet appointment in a later chapter.

Earlier in this chapter, I spent a lot of time on President Obama's foreign and domestic policies and actions. So, I would now like to do the same regarding President Trump's term and then, President Biden.

During his term, President Trump acted on many important issues, such as our VA hospital system, Keystone pipeline, and most importantly, the appointments of Neil Gorsuch, Brett Kavanaugh Amy Coney-Barrett to the Supreme Court. I cannot stress enough how important it was to select a nonpartisan judge to replace Judges' Scalia, Kennedy, and Ginsburg. Mr. Trump also demonstrated decisive leadership on a range of foreign affairs.

There is no question that his private sector experience and business acumen created positive inspiration to our economy and there are many economic indicators and data to support this.

Look at how just allowing current immigration laws to be enforced has had very positive results on illegal entry at our southern border.

So yes, President Trump has demonstrated presidential leadership. However, his erratic behavior at times only diminished his successes and further divided our country.

The unnecessary delays in his healthcare and tax reform initiatives were again due to the total dysfunction of congress and the many entrenched self-serving politicians that have been in office too long. This alone should have been a wakeup call for President Trump that he propel term limits to forefront of his agenda!

Mr. Trump promoted term limits many times during his campaign. However, after taking office, when he mentioned "term limits," it was immediately dismissed by Senate Majority Leader McConnell. I don't believe President Trump has ever brought it up again, which was very concerning!

More specifics and discussion on term limits in a later chapter.

As we evaluate these two Presidents, I strongly encourage my readers to truly assess the national news media's efforts to distort and omit the facts and, in many cases, present false narratives when covering Obama and Trump.

One of the reasons we are experiencing the crises I cite in this book is due to how corrupt and biased our news media has become. Along with these self-serving Washington politicians, their sycophants and those that try to influence our national politics, we see two standards of press coverage when comparing the coverage of Obama vs. Trump.

For those of you who don't remember the Obama years, just look at the press coverage of Biden. It is not only the same as their coverage of Obama, but even more biased and corrupt!

Let me further clarify my last statement. When I say biased and corrupt. I need to stress that in the majority of news accounts throughout Obama's two terms, many in our so-called mainstream news media never really criticized Obama when appropriate, but instead covered for his shortcomings and at the same time creating false narratives that he was successful.

This is prevalent again with Biden, even more so. They did just the reverse with Trump to a degree not seen before.

So now let's take a closer look at how Obama and Trump addressed similar foreign and domestic policy issues.

With regards to two of our most prominent adversaries, China and Russia, the difference could not be more different and alarming.

Look at how Trump pushed back on China with respect to a wide range of issues, especially on trade and how China's manipulation and our capitulation created years of unacceptable trade imbalances. He also openly questioned and raised concerns about China's stance on Hong Kong, Taiwan, and expansion in the South China Sea. Under Obama, China continued and accelerated its path forward of aggression and influences across the globe.

With Russia, consider what Obama did with respect to Vladimir Putin's expansion into Ukraine, seizing Crimea and outright aggression. While Obama provided only non-lethal support, Trump chose to supply the same but also lethal support through sales of military weapon systems. So, who was a stronger leader on China and Russia I think is very apparent.

With respect to ISIS and Iran, Trump did just the opposite of Obama's actions as I described earlier in this chapter. Trump's policies and actions lead to the end of ISIS's caliphate and halted America's involvement in the flawed JCPOA with Iran.

Also, consider Trump's ability in early 2017 to bring over 50 Arab countries together in a summit held in Saudi Arabia primarily to identify Iran's dangerous activities and desire to achieve complete dominance over the middle east and elsewhere. Who had the clearer leadership with these two examples?

Also, consider that nearing the end of Trump's fourth year we started to see additional Arab countries such as the UAE, Bahrain, Morocco, and Sudan normalize diplomatic relations with Israel. Trump also directed the US embassy in Israel to be moved to Jerusalem which many past presidents spoke about doing, but never did.

Lastly on foreign affairs, North Korea. While Trump did not achieve a major break through with Kim Jong Un, such as de-nuclearization, he did confront this threat much more directly than Obama and other former presidents by meeting with the North Korean leader. His first in Hanoi, followed by the summit in Singapore along with his third time at the DMZ, with a brief step on to North Korean soil.

I am sure that many Obama supporters will loudly refute these Trump initiatives as too much of a concession for a sitting US President to make with no assurances of any meaning full change by NK. However, Obama only practiced the same failed policy as former presidents with Washington speak, such as "strategic patience",

Trump showed his conviction to deal with this long un-resolved threat and meet this erratic leader face to face communicating US policy and conditions to reach a verifiable agreement. Their summit in Singapore did establish a very pro-active road map. However, Trump under-minded his accomplishments by his inability to not over embellish his relationship with Kim and the initiatives agreed to.

Trump's entire effort on NK was based on a clear message that he would not allow NK to strike America or our allies in the region and would use our military to act preemptively as well as maintain harsh sanctions.

I believe that Trump would have come much closer to solving this standoff in a meaningful way, not to mention removing our troops, if he had won a second term.

I also believe that this foreign policy initiative along with others, stalled, as foreign leaders started to calculate the 2020 presidential possibilities along with the political division and calls for Trump's impeachment.

President Trump did struggle with respect to his cabinet and white house appointments in terms of turnover, which was higher than recent former presidents. This did create additional confusion and chaos and certainly could have been prevented to a large degree.

With respect to domestic policy, Trump achieved many important initiatives with respect to our economy, such as job growth, low unemployment, sustainable low energy prices, business development and most importantly, an America first approach which incentivized companies to make more of their products here and bring jobs back to the US.

I ask my readers when reflecting on my comparison of Obama and Trump's foreign and domestic policy, to bear in mind that Obama had eight years to deal with the topics discussed while Trump had only four. Not to mention, that 2020 was adversely affected by the "COVID 19" pandemic and all the unnecessary restrictions simply due to the over politicization of this public health emergency.

In closing on President Trump, I firmly believe that his greatest impediment to a truly successful presidency was his own stubbornness and tendencies I described earlier. There were times when one would have to really wonder how he ever achieved success in life, when considering the lack of critical thought with many of his statements and beliefs.

Even with my statement in the prior paragraph, I still believe that if we place these presidents in a side-by-side comparison and then objectively, without any bias, I believe that my readers would see that President Trumps' four years were much better for our country than the eight years of President Obama. Please consider our country's future and please set the personalities of these two men to the side for this analysis.

President Trump's election was certainly a major event in the transition I speak to in this book and may be a turning point in choosing the correct path forward but has many pitfalls! As I stated at the outset, I believe the transition America now finds itself in, as we entered the twenty-first century, started with 9/11, along with the election of George W. Bush. So, I would be remiss if I didn't speak to his presidency.

In the 2000 presidential election, Mr. Bush won by a narrow margin. So close in fact that there was a major recount in Florida involving the infamous "hanging chad" debate.

It was finally settled by the US Supreme Court but never fully accepted by his opponent, then sitting US vice president Al Gore. It also was never fully recognized by those of Gore's political party and many in the media who continually questioned its legitimacy throughout Bush's two terms.

His opponents also called into question his election due to Gore winning the popular vote.

Sound familiar!

I am not going to spend a lot of time on President Bush's eight years in office. However, I will point out some very important aspects of his term in office.

In his first year in office, America suffered its greatest attack by a foreign terror group on our homeland like no other in our history, 9/11, where we lost almost three thousand innocent lives. America should never forget this horrific act by just nineteen Islamicjihadists willing to give their lives to kill as many as possible.

I believe this was the event that triggered the transition we currently find ourselves in. Yes, we did experience terrorist attacks prior to 9/11 but nothing as deadly and so organized.

Osama bin Laden and his terrorist group al-Qaeda were found to be responsible for this. Al-Qaeda had already demonstrated its lethality in prior attacks such as the ones in Africa in 1998.

In the 1998, then President Bill Clinton had the opportunity to take out Bin Laden, but hesitated and we lost our opportunity to possibly prevent 9/11. Another vivid example of presidential failure and a president with only his own political consideration in mind and nothing more.

The reason I cite George W. Bush's election as an event in our current period of transition is that I don't believe Al Gore would have guided America as well as President Bush did in the aftermath of 9/11.

In this aftermath, President Bush provided sound leadership in keeping America safe from further attacks of this nature and actively pursued these terrorists and those who supported their efforts.

He also provided inspirational guidance to America to not yield to fear and reminded every American to stand strong and never be intimidated by this evil ideology.

From that point forward, his presidency was heavily embroiled with military action in Afghanistan and in Iraq. As these conflicts continued, with many deaths and life-altering injuries, America became very impatient with these foreign involvements and rightly so!

I believe President's Bush continued reference to the "war on terror" confused and was too abstract for many Americans. Yes, we did go to war with a corrupt government in Iraq, America's strength prevailed, and that "war" was over very quickly. However, the protracted action in Iraq and sacrifice of American lives certainly can be questioned for its wisdom and will be for decades to come.

The conflict in Afghanistan continued until 2021!

I do not believe President Bush had the full spectrum of presidential leadership to effectively deal with these challenges. However, to be fair, his ability to find and implement the proper solutions was greatly diminished by the constant politicization practiced by a disingenuous Democrat Party and many in the media.

There must be political unity when America decides to go to war. Otherwise, there cannot be any national unity and again those disingenuous politicians only divide America, serving our enemies interest.

Mr. Bush also presided as president when America suffered a collapse of many of our financial institutions, leading to a serious long term, downward cycle to our economy, which certainly was another event in America's transition.

One very important failure by Presidential Bush was his inability and lack of meaningful attention to our southern border in dealing with unlawful entry and with respect to needed changes in our immigration system.

In closing on President Bush, I must say that he governed more from the status quo and big government. However, Mr. Bush has exhibited admirable character traits in his post-presidency, never really criticizing Obama or trying to inject himself into national policy. Although, he did inject his thoughts during the Trump presidency.

Compare his post-presidency to that of President Clinton and now Obama!

Presidential leadership in a post-presidency is also vital to America and should not be self-serving.

Now on to President Biden. As we find ourselves in President Biden's second year in office, it is now very apparent on what President Biden's vision for America is.

Not only do we see many policy flaws, but also serious character and leadership flaws as well.

Humility is so important to presidential leadership which obviously Biden lacks. A vivid example of this was his failure to acknowledge Trump's initiatives with respect to vaccine development, which came to be called "warp speed". This was an opportunity to rise above the divisive partisanship that consumes Washington and simply recognize this for the success it was, which occurred under Trump's direction.

Do you recall Mr. Biden's call for unity during his inaugural address and his first days in office? He may want to recheck the definition of unity as the lost opportunity I described in the last paragraph was neither unity nor inspirational for our nation, but rather only more destructive politics that continues to place America in peril.

Consider how President Biden's fixation on reversing Trump's initiatives in many instances has led to chaos and harm to America. Sure, when we have a presidential election and we have a change of party affiliation, we do have policy changes. But what Biden and those who influence him, wish to do is erase anything that Trump did or supported without any consideration for what is good policy for America.

This again is not leadership only petty partisanship. Smart leadership would be to build on whatever policy was working for America which would be unifying at the same time.

I again ask my readers to use that side-by-side comparison I spoke to earlier. But now add Biden to this analysis and closely evaluate policy vs. outcome and which policies and outcomes are right for America.

In the 2020 presidential election, over 70 million people voted for Trump. President Biden's radical agenda is now very apparent and is not concerned with those voices as well as the many Americans that voted for him.

President Biden's actions place America on a path of great risk, which threatens our prosperity and whether we will remain the single world power to ensure liberty and justice.

I implore my fellow citizens to watch Biden's actions very closely and not rely solely on a very biased press to understand the many crises facing our nation. Most importantly, inform themselves so that they see what is truly happening to our country.

His exit from Afghanistan was disgraceful! Sadly, it led to the unnecessary death and injuries to US military service members. Biden continues to diminish America's standing in the world, sending the wrong signals to those bad actors that wish to harm our country.

His foreign policy ineptness continues to destabilize the world, giving Russia, Iran and China further opportunities for continued aggression.

Look at how his incompetence and indecision created a window of opportunity for Russia to invade Ukraine. Consider all the loss of life and infrastructure as a result! If Biden had implemented sanctions early on instead of just threatening to do, this aggression may have been prevented. Instead, he played these silly word games about whether the sanctions were deterrents or not.

Why are we sending billions of dollars to Ukraine while America is experiencing a significant downturn in our economy?

Most importantly, America is suffering unnecessary hardships. Inflation is out of control with continuing cost increases for necessities that Americans need the most.

The stupidity of Biden and many in his administration is on full display as it relates to their push to eliminate fossil fuels through their out of touch initiatives and policy decisions.

His actions on stopping the construction of the Keystone pipeline and the southern border wall were only political and will take our country backwards, with no regard for America's economy or security.

The Biden administration is on average to reach two million illegal southern border crossings in each of first two years. This does include the so called got-aways, very alarming!

In closing on Biden, I must also encourage America to realize that President Biden may be compromised with respect to China due to his son Hunter and his dealings in China as well as with Ukraine, which started while Biden was the Vice President during Obama's two terms. This, along with the controversy over Hunter Biden's laptop and the references to his father must be fully and fairly investigated by the DOJ.

Please do not be distracted by many in politics and our media that this has been investigated, it has not!

A very alarming aspect of President Biden is that he is obviously experiencing cognitive decline. This along with the appearance of not being in charge and following the direction of others within his administration, has perilous consequences. Biden is completely out of touch with America and exhibits his arrogance and ineptness on a daily basis.

More on President Biden in later chapters.

So here we are, as we continue to experience a crisis of political leadership in this country, especially with respect to our presidency as well as these so-called congressional leaders I cited at the beginning of this chapter.

I will spend more time on those individuals holding these offices in a later chapter.

In closing this chapter, my effort is not to impugn Presidents Clinton, Bush, Obama, Trump or Biden and stress that I do not get any pleasure in criticizing any president, while in office or in their post-presidency.

However, I and every other American have the right to question and disagree with their actions and motives. And yes, criticize all our elected officials when we feel that they are not acting in the best interest of all Americans!

I continue to believe that America needs a true "citizen presidency." Please do not be confused by this statement; I am not referring to the requirement of US born citizenship to attain this high office.

What I am speaking to, is the need for our country to elect a president who is simply just an American citizen, not a politician (either current or former) and certainly not a billionaire celebrity. This citizen must be someone who has love of country (not oneself), great intellect, character, and conviction, and who has lived as the many million other Americans who expect genuine authenticity in the White House!

So please do not yield your right to free speech! Do not succumb to others and their attempts to influence your thought process, and please do not succumb to silent thought on your part, assuming our nation's leadership is not in crisis and does not deserve your full attention.

America needs active leadership from every citizen to solve this crisis. So please, do not sit on the sidelines!

CHAPTER 5

American Crisis Number Two—Political Correctness

This crisis, along with the other four cited in this book, have only worsened since I wrote my first book. Also prevalent with many of these crises, is the tactic to implore irrational emotion to stifle debate.

Two more recent notions within political correctness are the cancel culture and the woke culture.

So, what is political correctness, also referred to as PC?

Let's start with how dictionaries define it:

- Marked by or adhering to a typical progressive orthodoxy on issues involving especially ethnicity, gender, sexual orientations, or ecology.
- Demonstrating progressive ideals, avoiding vocabulary that is considered offensive, discriminatory, or judgmental, esp. concerning race and gender.

Why are we concerned with this as Americans? Or are we?

If this is progressive, are we moving forward or are we falling backward?

We have a political party in this country that self-identifies as progressives or progressive liberals, so does this represent all of America? Certainly not, unless you are part of this group.

So again, ask yourself, why are we concerned as Americans with political correctness? I believe we should be more concerned with "American correctness" and not just a set of subjective ideals promoted by a particular party and those who may agree with it. Is this not just another example of an individual or group of people trying to influence others who don't agree with them?

Sure it is, and it is also a serious attempt to target America's consciousness in a controlled way, with no room for debate, just strict adherence to their beliefs.

One of the reasons this is taking root in America is that, as discussed earlier, we have a media that in large part promotes this political party's agenda over others. This comes at us as targeted sound bites that root themselves in the minds of many Americans, without any validation.

Why? Well again, remember the silent thought tendency to just accept thought inspired by others without challenging the validity, whether it is accurate, and if it is just the biased views of others, meaning, it is just their opinion.

Have you noticed that more and more of these people who practice this deceit will say that not following their political correctness ideals goes against who we are as Americans? This is an attempt to shut down your analysis of their viewpoints and simply accept and follow their logic or be ridiculed.

Another tactic to accomplish their goal is to portray those who disagree as racist, sexist, biased or bigoted, unintelligent, or simply not as smart as they are, and not worthy of their respect. These are elitist views and do not depict American correctness.

Do not be fooled or misled by these tactics. We do not need a narrow viewpoint for how we should speak and live as Americans or for any one group insisting that all of America should subscribe to their views.

The difference between *American correctness* and *political correctness* is that American correctness does not restrict Americans in what they think or say, does not try to limit our freedoms, and seeks to preserve America's history, values, and traditions.

Have you ever watched one of these people that promote political correctness try to explain his or her narrow viewpoint or agenda?

They almost, literally, contort themselves before your eyes with all this distraction and distortion. Watch this closely!

Americans will treat other Americans correctly without the need for these narrow viewpoints or twisted values. American values have always been and will continue to be the guiding principles for America.

Sure, there are some in America who choose to hate and injure others, both in word and action, but we have laws in place to deal with this when appropriate.

We do not need political correctness disguised as a solution to combat this, when in reality, this is nothing more than a small group of people, unfortunately with national media influence, attempting to shut down debate or compromise to find an American solution, preferring that we just follow their twisted viewpoint on how Americans should act.

However, in post 2016 and 2020 presidential elections, we find this number increasing at an alarming rate.

An example of the incorrectness of political correctness was the controversy over the flying of the Confederate flag on the state's capital grounds after the senseless murder of nine black Americans in a church prayer meeting in Charleston, South Carolina, in June 2015.

A young man and a racist filled with hate murdered these nine innocents as he sat among them.

In the days that followed this horrific act, a photo was discovered of the killer holding a Confederate flag.

Immediately after, many started calling for the removal of the flag from the capital grounds, followed by knee-jerk reactions, such as calls to remove the flag from appearing in other southern states' flags, removing it from license plates, and removing a 1970s television show that featured a car with this flag on its roof.

And of course, President Obama weighed in, using this tragedy to speak about gun control. Sure, in his remarks, he also condemned the act and spoke to the loss for family and friends of the victims.

But ask yourself, was his effort only to disguise his remarks and only speak to his true motive, to again politicize a tragedy and promote his views on gun control? Think about it!

Now we know that killer's background check when purchasing the gun was handled incorrectly with respect to his criminal background investigation. If handled properly, he would not have been allowed to purchase a gun.

So again, we have a tragedy and senseless loss of life, and the real issues surrounding the case are ignored!

Why are we not focusing on why this young man's behavior and signs of hate and disorder were not acted on instead of this flag distraction or more gun control laws that did not cause this heinous act? Of course, those that use this tragedy to divert America's attention will never speak to this because that discussion does not fit into their narrative and narrow set of viewpoints.

An encouraging example of American correctness after this tragedy was how the citizens of Charleston, black and white alike, came together in prayer and unity, without riots or violent protests. After this incident, I heard a news interview conducted with Andrew Young, the former mayor of Atlanta, Georgia, and Civil Rights leader who marched alongside Dr. Martin Luther King Jr.

Mr. Young remarked, "Taking down the flag doesn't solve anything and had nothing to do with this act." He went on to say, "We should not wipe out our past but rather find ways to live together in the future."

He also commented that he would not trade one job for this flag. You see, Mr. Young is a leader who can reflect on our past injustices and at the same time choose to look forward to all Americans living together.

While this flag is not a great example of unity for America, it is, however, a part of America's history and has different meanings for different people, people who don't have hate in their hearts for other Americans. Their views are just as important as anyone else's.

Have you noticed that many of these people calling for political correctness are politicians? Ask yourself, are these politicians more concerned with the real issues at hand or their own political futures? We will discuss this in more detail in a later chapter.

Political correctness at its roots is a tactic to control freedom of speech, disguised as an enlightened way of thought. It is really only a way to promote silent thought!

Let's continue to analyze this.

I have always thought about why we feel the need to hyphenate certain race or ethnicities for some Americans. For example, when speaking of black Americans, we see those who practice PC use *African-American* at least once and then use *black American* in their remaining comments.

Why do we do this? I am of Italian, Irish, and German descent. Do I want to be referred to as an Italian-Irish-German-American or any variation of the three? Of course not!

While I am proud of my diverse heritage, I want to be simply identified as an American. I happen to be white. If I were black, does that make me any less of an American? Of course not, unless we allow that to happen through the attempts of others to divide us.

So, when speaking of Americans, why do we not refer to everyone in that way, instead of choosing to separate us or divide us along race identity? Are we not simply all part of the human race? I am not trying to oversimplify this, but we must move past this in unity.

Recently, I came across a poetic commentary written by an American icon, John Wayne. I was very moved by this, especially when hearing the audio, which you can easily find through an internet search.

Please read the following excerpt very carefully and truly evaluate its value in today's world, even though it was written in the early 1970s. I encourage you to find and read the entire writing.

"The hyphen, *Webster's Dictionary* defines, is a symbol used to divide a compound word or a single word.

So, it seems to me that when a man calls himself an Afro-American, a Mexican-American, Italian-American, an Irish-American, or Jewish-American, what he's saying is "I'm a divided American."

"United we stand . . . divided we fall. We're Americans . . and that says it all (John Wayne, circa 1972).

I first wrote this chapter over the Fourth of July holiday weekend, which provokes even more thought on this crisis, considering how our nation was born and has developed over the last 240-plus years. As many have stated, we are not a perfect union, but we are far and away the very best this world has ever known. Think of a world without America!

Throughout history and with all its success in conflicts with other nations, America has lost many brave lives yet has never sought to conquer the land of others but rather to secure and promote their liberty and sovereignty.

As previously stated, I am very concerned that many younger Americans, perhaps the Millennials, and Gen Z generations may take the greatness of this nation for granted, meaning that they might think our way life is so rooted that it is there forever.

All of us should realize that America's greatness has never been at greater risk for so many reasons.

I am also concerned that this same segment of our population might think it is okay to enlist political correctness as a viable solution to a perceived injustice or a better way of expression and not cherish those American institutions and values of greatness that have created the freedoms that they enjoy today.

America has changed over our very short history, but it should change with *American correctness* as the guiding light, not with such narrow viewpoints as *political correctness*, which reduces our greatness as a republic based on personal freedoms.

Let's look at another example of political correctness where its advocates were trying to have a football team change its name because they believe it is offensive to Native Americans, or American Indians. There's that division again!

Interesting enough, polls indicated that a majority of these proud Native Americans did not agree with this assertion. So why do these PC activists pursue this?

Well again, it is contrary to their narrow viewpoint, so it must be wrong, must be an injustice, and therefore must be done away with!

As discussed, many politicians pursue this. President Obama, who also pursues this behavior, allowed our US Patent and Trademark Office to remove the team's trademark protections for the use of this team's name. This was taken through our court system where activist judges upheld the USPTO's decision and again on appeal.

Fortunately, the ruling was later overturned by an appellate court. After a series of motions by both sides, the Supreme Court ruled the disparagement clause unconstitutional.

This convinced the five plaintiffs who brought the action against the Redskins to drop their claim.

In 2020, the team owners conceded and agreed to change the name after constant political and media pressure. There was also some financial pressure applied to this decision as well. Remember my earlier point that those who wish to target thought, take the long view, and never give up.

Yes, political correctness has also found its way into our nation's court system, with many judges ruling as activists, following their personal beliefs, ambitions, and agendas rather than being impartial and deciding cases solely based on our nation's laws.

As we conclude this chapter, I would like to stress that we are allowing a serious threat to our nation's safety when we allow political correctness to distract America from the real threat that radical Islamic terrorism is to our homeland.

Why did President Obama walk on eggshells when speaking around the real issue that some of the Muslim faith who are radical Islamists seek only to kill innocent Americans, either here or abroad?

Why did he insist on not identifying this enemy for who they are rather than describing them as "lone gunmen" or their attacks as "workplace violence"?

Even when the evidence was clear that those involved in these deadly acts against America were radical Islamic terrorists, President Obama remained silent and maintained his hardened ideology.

This is extremely puzzling given these enemies describe themselves as Islamic jihadists. This is not a reason to assume all the Muslim faith support this twisted perversion of Islam, but let's be clear-eyed here and understand that these radicals will kill not only those of non-Muslim faith but other Muslims as well!

Shutting down honest discussion of this problem and leaving Americans vulnerable, simply because of PC nonsense, has allowed dangerous radicalization within our borders to take root, which is exploited by our enemies.

Remember the tragedy where five of our military, four marines and one sailor, were targeted and murdered while working at two recruitment centers in Chattanooga, Tennessee. The killer was a foreign-born naturalized American citizen, twenty-four years old, who had been radicalized by "extremist and radical Islamic beliefs."

I bring this up because, again, President Obama refused to acknowledge this attack on our military and citizenry for what it really was and, adhering to political correctness, simply described it as random violence.

I believe Obama's reluctance was rooted in his determination to convince America that he and his policies had eliminated the threat of radical Islam and those who perpetrate it.

That could not be further from the reality of this threat.

It took President Obama five days to order our nation's flag to half-mast after this attack, and he did so only after public outcry and criticism.

The other concerning revelation of this tragedy was that our military members were not allowed to carry weapons while assigned to these recruitment centers.

These attacks on our military installations here in America are not a new occurrence, so why did President Obama and those he appointed to assess these threats to our nation not take the proactive and appropriate steps to ready these military targets to properly defend themselves?

We continued to suffer additional deadly attacks such as the ones in Orlando, Florida; San Bernardino, California; and others.

These are not simply lone wolves, as many would have you believe during the Obama years. This term was just another way to target thought and create an illusion that somehow this radical Islamic theology was somehow not connected to these worldwide Islamic jihadists.

ISIS and other groups of the same mind-set simply weaponized the internet and social media and found the way to increase its reach. If these were just one-offs, then why did many of the killers swear allegiance to ISIS leaders in the commission of their acts.

Those leaders that follow political correctness have failed our nation time and time again!

Is it not obvious that political correctness in these examples aid our enemies in their pursuits by suppressing thought and freezing our ability to take appropriate action?

So, you can see how our own poor decisions, if allowed to continue, threaten our freedoms that many in the world seek to eliminate. So again, the question: Why is political correctness a crisis for America today? Very simply, as you see from our discussions in this chapter, it creates division and not unity in America, which our enemies will and have exploited.

Our current state of transition is also affected by this crisis, and make no mistake about it, the eight years of Obama only worsened this crisis.

Two more examples.

Consider the episode where a professional football quarterback refused to place his hand on his heart during our national anthem and instead just kneeled on one knee.

What this young man fails to understand is that his action n o t only disgraces himself but disgraces and dishonors the men and women who gave their lives to safeguard his freedoms to disagree, not dishonor America.

His actions were in response to his personal beliefs on race relations and should be respected, but his actions were not appropriate while a member of his team and his requirements as an employee on the field but most importantly his behavior as an American. He incorrectly conflated two distinctly different issues. I and many other Americans would gladly stand with him to confront any racism when found.

Also, consider the many instances of those who insist on changing the names of schools and public highways and the removal of statues or plaques—all because they supposedly offend so many, when, it is only a pretense by those with narrow viewpoints who only wish to control free speech.

Erasing our country's history will not rewrite it. It will only prevent many in today's America and those future generations to not truly understand America's struggles and development as the greatest nation on earth.

This cancel culture continued through the Trump term. However, he did push back on this throughout his time in office. Instead of continuing this irrational and divisive behavior, why don't we stop the cancel culture that hurts America and instead do the following.

Why don't we cancel poverty and homelessness!

Why don't we cancel failing schools and teachers!

Why don't we cancel gun and gang violence across America!

Why don't we cancel failing politicians at all levels of government!

Why don't we cancel drug abuse and deaths across America!

Why don't we cancel illegal entry into America!

And yes, why don't we cancel broken families across America!

With respect to this woke culture, I implore my fellow Americans to reject this irrational wokeness, but rather get very woke as it relates to the true crises facing America!

Political correctness of any type seeks to diminish the greatness of America.

That simple!

If we don't resist those tendencies of silent thought, as it relates to this crisis, we may never realize what is at stake for America.

I am not suggesting, as I have stated in earlier chapters, that you allow this to consume every aspect of your daily life, but it will take your attention and analysis to truly understand its potential for disastrous consequences for our nation.

Remember, American correctness will win the day and will provide the guidance we need as a nation!

CHAPTER 6

American Crisis Number Three— Race Relations in America

This is the crisis that concerns me the most at this time in our history as a nation.

In the twentieth century, we were fortunate to have Dr. Martin Luther King Jr. come along at the right place and time for our country. MLK was an American leader, as much as he was a leader for the civil rights movement of the 1960s.

Not only was he a leader of quality, but he was truly an inspirational leader with the fortitude and conviction of his beliefs. I still get goose bumps every time I hear his "I Have a Dream" speech.

MLK created an awakening for this country, but even with all the roadblocks and humiliation he encountered, he still chose to lead peaceful protests in the spirit of unity, not division. He was truly an American hero.

We need a Martin Luther King for the twenty-first century, and we need it now!

Sadly, President Obama could have been this leader, but as I said earlier, he has chosen a different path than MLK as it relates to race relations in America.

I know some will disagree and say that he was elected as our president and not to champion a civil rights issue or race relations and that he had to govern all of America, certainly not choosing sides. Well, let's think about that.

I would say to those who challenge my assertion, if this were true, that he as our president should not have involved himself in race relations, then why did he pick and choose when he did inject himself—and only then in highly racially charged incidents across America?

Unfortunately, President Obama chose a path that divided Americans along race. He injected himself not to unify but rather to divide.

MLK sought to look to the future where race would no longer be a wedge between Americans, and he urged America to consider the content of our character and not the color of our skin. Sound familiar?

Martin Luther King and all of those who stood with him, through unwavering conviction, overcame the institutional racial discrimination that existed in America. They set the stage for future generations to build on that success and move this country forward in unity.

Many in today's America who are in a position to unite and build on prior achievements have failed these courageous leaders of the 1960s.

Unfortunately, some who stood with MLK still choose only to focus on the past injustices when speaking to today's America instead of speaking to the future that MLK envisioned.

This country has memorialized MLK with a national monument in the form of his statue and a national holiday to celebrate his birthday. This will forever be a tribute to him, standing alongside America's other great monuments and leaders.

Is this not a tremendous achievement for a country that was so troubled by the institutional racism of the twentieth century?

So why do we not take advantage of these tangible achievements to shape the correct path forward as a united America?

I believe that if MLK were here to see the lack of progress after all that he sacrificed, he would say, "Don't just celebrate me on one day in January every year, but rather embrace my spirit of unity every day and move forward to vanquish racism of all kinds in America!"

President Obama was among those able to have a profound and positive influence on this crisis, but he failed and chose to look backward and not find ways to move forward to unite in an inspiring way as MLK did.

He insisted on highlighting only the racial wrongs of the past while always trying to tie these wrongs to present-day interactions between black and white Americans.

He was especially outspoken and critical of our nation's law enforcement when we saw an officer interact with someone in the black community. Facts or no facts, he insisted on citing racism as the only reason for police interaction with blacks.

Did you ever notice that Obama only spoke briefly and infrequently about the enormous strides forward that this country has accomplished?

Ask yourself, what were his real motives?

He surrounded himself with others who also failed to unite, such as Al Sharpton, who self-identifies as a civil rights leader. When have you ever heard this individual try to unite America—all America and not just black America?

And let there be no mistake, Al Sharpton does not try to unite black America but rather incite black America toward anger and hatred. This individual is not a leader for America, and for a president to validate him as a leader is counterproductive and disingenuous.

So why is all this happening? Well, sadly, as I stated earlier, President Obama chose to politicize every crisis we encountered, meaning he used these crises to promote his political party's agenda and ideology over the well-being of this nation.

Let me stress that I am not being naive as it relates to the practice of politics by politicians! However, all Americans must think clearly when evaluating the use of this tactic in terms of race relations, which can harm and stifle American greatness.

A president should be the last to employ this tactic if he or she is truly an American leader.

Let's go back for a minute to my assertion that President Obama could have been instrumental in the creation of an MLK moment for the twenty-first century.

Our black communities in the inner cities of America are in great turmoil. If President Obama had spent just a small amount of his time—in a consistent, well-intentioned way—finding ways to inspire those who felt left out of society, we would be further ahead rather than further behind with respect to racial tensions in our country.

Think of it. America had just elected its first black president. Who is better than he to excite those in the black community who felt disenfranchised from America?

Who better than he to inspire people to challenge themselves to rise above the thoughts of racial inequality?

Who better than he to speak honestly about the greatness of a country that, after all the racial struggles of the twentieth century, elected a black man as president in the twenty-first century?

Who better than he to speak to those who chose the path of crime and self-destruction to instead choose the path of hard work and personal responsibility?

I am deeply disappointed that there have been so many lost opportunities for all of America to rise above these challenges simply because a few so-called leaders choose politics or division over meaningful conversation and change.

So why has America allowed this to happen? Many Americans have just accepted those powerful sound bites of hate and mistrust rather than truly think through this problem.

America must stop speaking in terms of minority and majority with respect to the races of its citizens. This is only exploited by those who seek to divide and attempt to diminish America's progress in overcoming racial tensions.

Those that target America's consciousness to promote racial strife and division solely to advance their own agendas and personal ambitions are despicable and should be removed from the discussion.

Look at some of the cases during Obama's term in office, between a white police officer and a black American, which tragically ended in the death of the black American.

In these examples, consider how all the misinformation and distrust has further divided America.

Consider how all the deception perpetrated by some has only created more rioting, more destruction of property, more hate, more distrust, and a further breakdown of societal norms.

I want to stress that many of those in our news media have done nothing to expose these bad actors at both the national and local levels of government. In many cases, they choose to follow the same twisted narrative of those who choose division.

Remember how insidious it is to ignore the critical facts and simply promote falsehoods as credible news accounts of these life-changing events in our society.

Additionally, look at how these same purveyors of division seek only to discredit our nation's law enforcement without any effort to honor these same men and women who provide our public safety.

This deception only further raises tensions and adds to the violence!

I am always motivated to stay positive that America can solve this crisis when I hear blacks speak to this crisis in an honest and profound way. They attempt to speak to the minds and hearts of all Americans, not just black America.

These leaders might be just an everyday American trying to live his or her life to the fullest. They could be local or national politicians, or they could be people in education, law enforcement, or the clergy. Whoever they are, they should be heard by all of America and without others trying to silence their voices.

I mentioned before that if you criticized President Obama and you were white, many, especially in our media, would label you as a racist.

Have you noticed that when a black person states a position or promotes a narrative that is different from those who seek to divide us along race, he or she is called some of the most vicious names imaginable. They are referred to as "Uncle Tom," "not authentically black," "sellout," and on and on.

These black Americans would rather lead as Martin Luther King Jr. did and look for ways to bring us forward rather than backward, which, if we allow it, could destroy the nation we all love and cherish.

These same black Americans have not forgotten America's past or racial struggles, but they would rather look to the future for ways to bring America together and not simply wipe out our experiences. Unfortunately, pursing racial strife and perceived racial injustice has become a way of life in this country for some who choose to profit from it or gain national prominence. Some in politics use this division solely to create voting blocs to ensure their reelection.

What I just described in the last paragraph is a great example of how some seek to manipulate thought to further their personal ambitions when they have no real interest in solving this crisis or helping the people affected. They are only interested in our mindless agreement with their views—and only their views!

Think about these motivations and ask yourself, are these purveyors of racial strife in any way concerned with solving this crisis? Sadly, no!

Those in politics and those so-called civil rights leaders shape their messages to promote despair and distrust among the very people that are hurt the most. Yet sadly, these same people believe these so-called leaders are acting in their best interest.

A person who chooses to stay uninformed and not seek the truth, who instead blindly accept falsehoods, is the most vulnerable. Unfortunately, there is a large segment of these individuals of every race in our country.

As silent thought becomes the norm, the greater the risk that our thought will harden in place, and what we see, hear, and read will not penetrate our consciousness. You can see examples of this throughout your day if you pay close attention to exchanges between people.

Do not kid yourself; some politicians and those who support them will take advantage of this and exploit it to the fullest extent possible.

After the tragedy in Ferguson, Missouri, the phrase "black lives matter" became a recurring statement by blacks, whites, activists, and politicians, with many in the media repeating it as well.

How many of these same politicians, civil rights leaders, activists, and those in the media have you heard express the same concerns for all the senseless killing as a result of black-on-black crime in our inner cities across this nation? Their silence is staggering!

Why was the tragedy in Ferguson, where a white police officer shot a young black man, more important to these same so-called leaders and some in the media?

Why do they speak so loudly about this and stay silent about the loss of black lives when taken by other blacks?

Do those black lives not matter?

This loss of life does not matter to those with personal or political agendas and those who do not have any concern for a unified American agenda!

A serious barrier to honest conversation about this crisis is that if you do not agree, you might be labeled as a racist or a sellout, which shuts downs debate very quickly.

Many Americans simply choose to sit back and hope for change but do very little else to engage in this discussion.

I believe the way we start to solve this crisis is for us to look only to leaders, both black and white, who believe in unity, not division. As stated earlier, thought for many of us has really hardened!

Those who promote silent thought (meaning they don't want you to challenge their viewpoints, wanting you to simply accept them) have so inflamed racial tensions that not only do people's thoughts harden but their hearts harden as well!

The keys to unlock this are difficult to find, but equally difficult is to reestablish the trust between different races. This American problem has gone unaddressed for quite some time.

However, when speaking openly about it, you can look to many personal success stories that have lifted many from despair to fully enjoying the American dream in a color-blind society.

The opportunities for meaningful change when President Obama took office were plentiful but were not acted on. Additionally, throughout his tenure in office, he was provided with additional opportunities to act in of all America's interest.

Time and time again, Obama used these opportunities to further divide America in a very deceptive way, only citing income inequality and racial inequality to build a voting bloc that sees race through one lens.

He and those who supported his motives don't believe in finding ways to expand life's opportunities for these segments of our population. They prefer to promote despair and envy, which can only lead to distrust and hate.

These politicians that promote racial strife believe that they can manipulate many in our black community, especially in our inner cities, by providing government programs that hold people in place rather than providing pathways to self-reliance and personal growth. These same politicians, when speaking about adding more people to welfare programs, act as if it is a badge of honor. This is not something to celebrate; rather, these leaders should be embarrassed for failing to lead all of America and find ways to lift those out of poverty and despair.

I am not understating the importance of our country being a compassionate nation and having appropriate government programs and safety nets for the poor and those caught in an endless cycle of despair.

But you see, some of our politicians and civil rights leaders want to create and continue dependency, which they believe will maintain a reliable voting bloc, which will keep these politicians in office and these civil rights leaders relevant.

I cannot stress this enough. These political tactics are some of the most destructive to our nation's unity more so than any other crisis facing our country.

Is it any wonder that we continue to see rioting and unrest in these communities? As I stated earlier, when one's thought and heart harden, despair and distrust will settle in, and violence will erupt.

Look back at the rioting and destruction in Baltimore, Maryland, after six police officers, three white and three black, were accused of causing the death of a black man while in police custody.

In Baltimore, at the time of this unrest, you had a black mayor, a black police commissioner, and a black state's attorney. Yet these protestors still felt the need to riot and destroy property. Why?

This provides one of the most vivid examples of how those who seek to manipulate our thoughts and advance their own political and personal ambitions and agendas can so easily influence others to reject objective thought, the rule of law, and basic common sense. This was another example of where some used this tragedy to promote distrust of law enforcement, which only accomplished more violence and destruction.

The mayor of this city, in a press conference during the unrest, actually stated, "We provided space for those who wished to destroy the space to do that," then tried to insist that she did not make this statement.

She also instructed her police department to not engage the rioters and hold in place, functionally telling law enforcement officers to stand down. Many officers were injured as a result, and there was extensive damage to private and public property.

Baltimore's police commissioner denied these nonengagement orders given to his police force during these protests.

This mayor also made the comment that this incident was a difficult balancing act.

Really!

What allowed this situation to spiral out of control? Was it due the incompetence of this mayor?

Is the answer not obvious?

Thankfully, Maryland's governor stepped in and called up the National Guard to assist in bringing order to a volatile situation.

Baltimore's mayor did not provide leadership, and while observing her handling of this incident, it was apparent how arrogant she was and how unfit she was to deal with this unrest. I do wonder if she had any communication with President Obama's administration during this protest and rioting.

Baltimore's state's attorney also displayed her incompetence in the early stages of this incident, acting more as an activist against perceived racial injustice than as a state's attorney that should only be concerned with the pursuit of legal justice for all.

Through her remarks, it became obvious that she was more concerned with personal ambitions and her own agenda than truly pursuing the justice that is demanded of the office she held.

What have these political leaders and those of their political party done while in office to foster trust in our legal system by those who instead chose violent protest and rioting?

Why didn't any of these political leaders in Baltimore attempt to speak to those rioting, to appeal for respect of law and order?

In the weeks that followed, Baltimore experienced very high numbers of black-on-black killings. Why would this happen?

Have these people who choose crime been emboldened by the ineptitude of Baltimore's leaders during those protests and riots?

Was the morale in Baltimore's police department so low because of this mayor's behavior and her lack of support for these brave men and women that they chose not to police actively and look the other way?

Think about it. Other police departments across the nation, such as the NYPD, have also lost confidence in their mayors for the same reasons.

There is no question that our nation's law enforcement agencies can experience neglect or discriminatory behavior by some in their ranks, but this is the rare exception and not the norm when dealing with all Americans, white and black alike.

These incidents are dealt with as they occur with disciplinary action and retraining, but we should be certain that our law enforcement members are policing themselves as well as our communities.

Our leaders, both local and national, must support law enforcement and speak strongly to all citizens that our law enforcement professionals are there for the common good and must be respected at all times.

Here again was another opportunity for President Obama to present a positive message to those in Baltimore that felt the need to pursue a life of crime and violence instead of being law-abiding citizens.

This was occurring within minutes of our White House, a forty-five-minute drive, or even quicker in Marine One.

But again, he failed to act as a leader to inspire and instead remained silent!

Even if President Obama did not want to concede on his insistence to only highlight racial tensions, why not take this opportunity to speak to those who have abandoned family values, personal growth and responsibility and encourage them to instead embrace these ideals?

Why would he not use his advantage of being the first black president and his bully pulpit to reach as many black Americans as possible with a positive message of hope and inspiration rather than the continuing theme of despair and victimization?

Why would he not want to inspire as many black Americans as possible to take the path that he followed of hard work, perseverance, and sacrifice, then highlight the results of these choices with his personal successes, strong family values, and of course, his being elected the forty-fourth president of the United States of America?

Please do not let anyone attempt to convince you otherwise or allow him or her to target your thoughts with distractions and excuses.

Every American should question Obama's motives and realize how destructive his message of division has been and how his silence has harmed so many who needed positive reinforcement and the courage to change the paths they are following and reject crime and violence.

I firmly believe that the root of the violence in our communities starts with the breakdown of the family unit. Every American begins his or her life in innocence and without any of these antisocial tendencies.

However, if our children are not raised with the care and love required to instill life's critical values and morality, along with the unity and equality that MLK embraced, they will not take the correct path toward adulthood. They will fail and fall into a cycle of dependency and crime.

Even if a parent is doing his or her best to raise his or her children, oftentimes it is counteracted by outside influences. For example, a struggling single parent is trying to speak to his or her adolescent or young adult child about life experiences, personal responsibilities, and how to behave in and outside the home.

Yet all this child or young adult is exposed to outside of the home is an onslaught of distorted views that promote distrust and despair and speak only about racial inequality, income inequality, and distrust for law enforcement!

In addition to these distorted viewpoints, these children and young adults become addicted to not only drugs in some cases but also the perceived easier path of crime, dealing drugs, and a gangster or thug mentality.

America must deal with this issue; we cannot ignore it. It will not go away, and we must not fail!

Think back to the Michael Brown tragedy in Ferguson, Missouri. Who failed this young man in his formative years? What allowed this young man to think it was okay to steal and, most importantly, that it was okay to fight with a police officer for the officer's gun and assault the police officer along with his friend?

During the entire incident and the violent unrest that followed, how many times did you hear anyone asking questions about why this young man's path did not take him in a different direction other than crime and having no respect for law enforcement?

The silence was alarming.

Please do not be distracted by those who deny or talk around this assertion by saying that Michael Brown was victimized by racial discrimination.

Unfortunately, this is just one tragedy along with so many other senseless deaths occurring in our communities.

Does the fact that these inner-city communities are no longer spoken about in the press or by those purveyors of racial strife and division mean that the violence, crime, and despair have ceased?

Of course not. So again, where are these same individuals that shouted so loudly that black lives matter?

They are not interested in these deaths because they do not further their disingenuous agendas and personal ambitions. Sadly, lives are still being lost at alarming rates, yet now these lives are no longer visible.

Cities such as Chicago and Baltimore continue high rates of gun violence and death. Where are the solutions!

Please consider the high number of abortions among blacks in our inner cities. Do these black lives not matter as well?

Look at the unacceptably high rates of unemployment among blacks in our inner cities.

Look at the unacceptably high rates of poverty and crime among these same Americans.

Let's be clear. The racial tensions and crime that exist in our inner cities, especially in the black communities across our nation, require a unified approach by many in America in order to overcome.

We drastically need a catalyst to ignite a true determination to move forward in the ways MLK dreamed of and fought for!

This catalyst must be so powerful, it can soften the hardened thoughts and hearts of those that follow the path of self-destruction so that positive reinforcement for change has a chance to enter their consciousness.

We must ask ourselves, what political party is in control of these cities where the crime and racial unrest is the highest across our nation? Are we allowing political agendas to make this problem worse?

We must stop this endless cycle of dependency by many in these inner-city communities and motivate those trapped there to reach for greater fulfillment in life rather than accepting the status quo. Government dependency, without understanding or believing in the values of personal responsibility, hard work, and self-worth, will only create more dependency, despair, and envy, followed by crime in many cases.

Ask yourself, why did President Obama undermine the work requirements for those on public assistance through executive decisions?

Did he and his supporters really believe that this policy to eliminate work requirements would promote greater personal responsibility?

Sadly, no! They intentionally created more dependency, believing that in doing so, it will further ensure that those affected will vote for them and their failed policies.

Please evaluate this honestly. How could dependence on government handouts ever be more rewarding than the experience of personal independence and all the successes that can follow?

Those trapped in this generational cycle of despair—but are not committing any crime and are struggling to find the pathway to a better standard of living—are in a constant state of fear of the extreme violence and drugs that have overtaken their neighborhoods. Those disingenuous community leaders and politicians and those in the news media that only denigrate and call into question the motives and character of those in law enforcement are making a very bad situation that much worse.

If we lose control over law and order, we are sure to fail as a nation!

Let's be clear. There are some that seek only to commit violent crime and reject established social norms, and these individuals should be dealt with firmly and fairly within our justice system.

However, we cannot fail to look at the root cause for this breakdown of personal conduct and the bad choices that follow and take actions to reverse this downward spiral toward self-destruction.

We must address these root causes and deal with those that break our laws at the same time. One without the other will not give us the space and time to overcome these problems for black and white alike.

When we look at the nonviolent segments of our society with respect to race, we see differences between our older and younger generations.

Of our older generation, let's say the baby boomers and older, many have experienced or witnessed racial discrimination in their lifetimes.

I would like to believe that many older Americans recognize that this period was very difficult for blacks in America but have also seen the many successes in eliminating racism, starting from the days of MLK to our present time.

They also believe in America's determination to eradicate racism of any type in our nation and allow America to heal and move forward in unity.

Sadly, though, there are those who still harbor hate and mistrust, both among whites and blacks. Their thoughts and hearts remained hardened, in a place and time that no longer exists.

They will not allow themselves to find the honest and productive path forward—not to forget these past injustices but rather look to the future in unity.

In all fairness, it is very difficult for anyone to look forward when you have so many so-called political and civil rights leaders, as well as many in our news media, acting as if racism is still dominating our society.

And they are doing so for all the wrong reasons, as discussed earlier in this chapter.

Sure, America will always experience some random act of discrimination, as we are a very diverse nation, and there will always be someone who hates another simply because of a different ethnicity or color or faith.

I believe through attrition we will resolve the stubbornness of some of our older generation, as some may never change their minds, no matter what message they are listening to.

Our younger generations do not view race the same way our older generations do but are still very susceptible to targeted thought by those who profit from division and identity politics.

If our country were left to evolve naturally, without this insidious intervention by narrow-minded politicians and so-called civil rights leaders who only foster hate and division, our younger generations would overcome this problem.

It may take another generation or two to fully solve it, but I believe it is doable.

Is it not encouraging whenever you see our young children, black and white, playing together without ever thinking of race or color?

Of course, they wouldn't, unless they are encouraged to do so by others who wish to target their thought with hate and dishonesty rather than love and inspiration.

Sure, our young children probably notice a difference in color but not through the lens of any racial bias.

You also see this in our younger generation at an older age as well. They simply don't consider race as a barrier to relationships and pursuing mutual interests as friends or colleagues.

Our thought creates lenses through which we see others. Unfortunately, in many cases our lenses do not flip forward, allowing the color-blind lens to flip into place.

President Trump did try to address this crisis during his time in office. However, early on, Trump was accused of being a racist, which many in the media perpetuated. This was just one of many distortions that continued throughout his presidency and further divided this country.

I encourage my readers to evaluate the validity of these distortions fairly and factually. As stated earlier, Trump had flaws, but many of these attacks were simply politically driven.

One important evaluation with respect to policy outcomes between Obama and Trump, would be to look at key economic indicators among minorities.

Please look at the unemployment levels, wages, both salaried and most importantly hourly wages. Compare Obama's term after eight years to that at of Trump's four years.

Now, with President Biden in office, sadly we find an even a greater desire than Obama to divide this country along the lines of race.

The fact that President Biden would stand before the American people and state that there is systemic racism in this country, not only illustrates how uninformed he is, but also tells us that he will only continue the same falsehoods with no concern to truly address this crisis.

Make no mistake in thinking through this crisis, the purveyors of racial strife and division will continue to target all Americans, especially our younger generation, with these divisive tactics to promote distrust and hate.

I want to stress that I know that some may disagree with my assertions on this crisis and argue that my thoughts are too simplistic. Please challenge their viewpoint and remember that when honesty guides us, the solutions are simple and straightforward!

We just need the courage to act and believe in America's greatness to overcome this challenge.

So, in closing this chapter, I encourage those who want to be part of an MLK moment for our country, please step forward!

President Obama could still be an important part of this moment in his post-presidency if he is truly concerned about this crisis. However, I tend to doubt his willingness to address this honestly.

President Obama, America is still waiting!

CHAPTER 7

American Crisis Number Four—Politics in America

As we prepare to discuss this crisis, I ask you to reflect on the previous chapters on the crises facing America, looking at how interconnected they really are.

In this chapter, we will see how our politics and those who hold political office can have a dramatic effect on the causes and solutions for the crises that I have identified in this book.

If I were to say, "We the people need to take back Washington"— by Washington, I mean our government in Washington, DC "We the people need to change our political system," do these sound like radical or extremist comments?

They may, and I can understand if you think they are. They are not radical or extreme in the sense that they would result in an act of violence or not following the rule of law.

However, these are radical and extreme statements that express the seriousness of this crisis. Our American political system is in crisis and requires the attention of every American.

It is extremely important for every American to understand that we are not just a democracy; we are also a constitutional republic, where power is vested in its citizens and not the politicians we elect. It is also important to remember that just because a majority of politicians pass a law, we should not assume it is lawful under our constitution, simply due to a majority decision in congress followed by the signature of our president.

When considering a US Supreme Court decision, here again, just because a majority of nine justices decide to uphold or strike down a matter before them, we should not assume their decision is lawful under our constitution.

However, this is difficult to challenge due to how our constitution was written, which makes their decision the law of the land.

We will speak about our US court system, including the US Supreme Court and how politicized it has become, later in this chapter.

How often do you think about politics, either local or national? Daily? Only occasionally? Only leading up to an election? Briefly after hearing or reading a short sound bite? Or really never at all?

I would like to stress that simply allowing a questionable sound bite from a newscast or the front page of newspaper to enter your consciousness is not thinking about politics but rather is allowing the opinions of others to possibly form your opinion, which you may or may not repeat as if it were your opinion.

Remember the concepts of silent thought and spontaneous, targeted, and stubborn thought and how damaging they can be if you do not challenge your thought process and the validity of what you allow to enter and take root in your consciousness.

Let me stress that I am not judging anyone's decision to accept these opinions or so-called news accounts if you happen to agree with them. Every American is free to think and believe anything he or she chooses to.

However, my goal, as stated several times earlier, is to promote critical thought analysis when considering the crises discussed in this book.

So back to whether we are really thinking about politics. Why would we, especially when for many of us it appears in the abstract and not worthy of our daily thought activities?

Yet we should understand that everything in life that we enjoy and everything we do not is in one way or another driven by local and national politicians and their actions.

As we continue this chapter, we will focus more on national politics and those politicians. However, please do not fail to consider your local and state political institutions. Some are working in their community's best interest, but many are in crisis.

Local politics that succeed is a result of them being closer to the people they represent. But make no mistake—unless we hold them accountable, they will move further from the people they represent and closer to serving only themselves.

When we consider politics and the actions of specific politicians in our daily lives, it is important that we understand that they are not always acting in our best interest or that of our nation.

Then whose interest are they concerned with?

Is it their own political careers, their respective party affiliation and its ideology, special-interest groups who donate to their campaigns, or the leaders in their respective chambers such as the US Senate and House of Representatives?

Yes, to all—and probably other reasons that we are not aware of but are certainly not in our best interest.

But ask yourself, who elected these individuals to their respective offices?

We the people, right? Well, not necessarily!

So why would they not consider only our interests and those of our nation when fulfilling the duties of their office?

Several reasons.

The biggest and most disturbing reason is that many of our politicians have forgotten and really choose to ignore that they are public servants elected to office to serve our interests rather than serving their own personal ambitions and careers.

They have forgotten or fail to recognize that public service was not meant to be a career path to enrich oneself while in office and, more specifically, after leaving office.

Time and time again, we have seen newly elected politicians enter their office with the highest of ethical standards and transparency with the American public, but either they are corrupted and then follow those who hold power, or they try to lead and remain true to their higher standards of conduct.

Unfortunately, those that try to lead and serve the interests of those who elected them are marginalized by the corrupt nature of our current political system.

So given the recent political slogan "Drain the Swamp," these politicians simply become "Swamp Things."

It is important to understand how the targeted thought of others plays a very large role in our voting decisions, especially by those who seek higher offices, such as state governors, those in congress, and our president.

Not only do these politicians target our thought, but all of those who support them, and their party do as well.

Also, as we have discussed earlier, depending on their party affiliation, many in our news media support one party over the other rather than just impartially reporting on every candidate and public policy.

As each of these campaigns move through their primary contests and get closer to Election Day, we are barraged with endless print and television ads, along with the opinions of political pundits and, in many cases, biased opinions disguised as news.

All of this is done in an effort to persuade you to cast your vote in their favor.

Ask yourself, isn't it interesting how visible we are to these politicians when they need our vote but so invisible to them after they win election?

If we allow others to target our thought process and then cast our vote without validating whether it is in our best interest and that of our nation, who is really voting?

So, you see, we have not really elected this politician. Sure, we are the ones who entered the polling place and cast the vote.

But if we simply yielded to outside influences without spending time evaluating a candidate's true motives and qualifications, the ballot we cast is not ours but is that of someone else who directed our action in their interest!

We have now become their instrument to achieve their objectives, and in doing so, we have put at risk our identity and our freedoms under our constitution.

Let's be clear here. To win, politicians must target our thoughts, and that's okay. We want those asking for our vote to explain their reasons for seeking office and to present their qualifications for us to examine.

However, we must be very discerning when considering these national elections and resist the temptation to simply accept quick sound bites to form our decision regarding whom to vote for.

Our greatest right and our most important responsibility as Americans are to cast our vote as a well-informed citizen with not only our interest in mind but serious concern for the interests of this great nation.

I strongly encourage you not to vote simply on a straight party line, meaning that we do not necessarily consider the candidate and instead only vote for everyone within a certain party affiliation, such as Democrat, Republican, libertarian, or Independent.

To do so is just another example of how our vote can be manipulated. Consider how many in certain parties try to take advantage of this tendency by demeaning others simply because they identify with a particular party.

They use this tactic to unnecessarily divide America while at the same time believing they will create additional power and control for their party through practicing identity politics.

Additionally, they exploit this tendency and know that a certain percentage of voters will cast their vote for party affiliation rather than consider all candidates fairly.

The days where a political party has earned and deserves our faith and trust are nonexistent in today's political system. Unfortunately, many of today's politicians and those who support them play fast and loose with the truth.

Please pay special attention to politicians and those who support them when listening to their comments; they only demean their opponents instead of honestly debating the issue with them.

Those who employ this tactic are very good at deception and do not want an honest exchange of ideas!

Politicians, especially those in Washington, DC, have shown us many times over that they will put their own personal ambitions above those that have elected them—and by extension our country.

Politics by its nature creates division and opposition, which is why we must pay more attention to this crisis at this time, more than at any other time in our nation's history!

We must take the dramatic steps that will change our American political system. But we can only accomplish this with a unified approach and with the attention of all of America.

Many of our politicians have become so entrenched in their respective office and party that they are now failing America with far greater frequency. Remember my comment about how we become invisible after they secure our vote. Think about it!

Think about all the policy positions stated and promises made during a campaign, and then after they are elected, consider how many of these politicians actually do what they promised and then only engage in excuses and double-talk.

When considering the major challenges facing our country, we must no longer readily accept their actions and words as correct and trustworthy but rather dissect their actions and words in-order to determine their true intent and value.

I know this all sounds very cynical on my part, but we must come to the realization that our government in Washington, DC, has become totally dysfunctional and in many cases very corrupt.

The reasons for this are many. However, the genesis for this dysfunction is that everything is so politicized. Contradictory, right? Not when you consider that what I mean by the overpoliticization of our government is that these so-called leaders in Washington only take actions with their own party and political futures in mind. This is why at this point every American must resist the tendency of silent thought, meaning that we have to find the time to challenge our thought processes in order to truly understand the nature of this crisis.

To only accept the opinions of a small group of politicians in Washington, those who support them, and those in our news media with political motives transfers control of our destiny to those few in Washington!

If we do not have an honest conversation with ourselves about how much we understand and what we do not understand about national politics, we will never find ourselves in a position of strength and confidence to deal with this crisis effectively.

Please do not ignore this crisis and expect someone else to solve the problem!

Believe me, these politicians exploit this apathy on our part and will only continue to deceive until they realize that we have taken a proactive mind-set to hold them accountable as public servants.

Have you ever wondered why politics in Washington has to be so complicated?

Well, it does not have to be.

Let's go back to the national leaders I referenced in an earlier chapter. In addition to the presidency, we had John Boehner (until the fall of 2015), the speaker of the House of Representatives, and Nancy Pelosi, the minority leader in the House of Representatives.

Then in the US Senate, we have Mitch McConnell, the majority leader, and Harry Reid, the minority leader, who decided not to seek reelection in 2016. He was succeeded by Chuck Schumer, another partisan-entrenched politician.

Then you have several others in both chambers that compose their respective leadership teams.

These so-called leaders in the House of Representatives and the US Senate are collectively at the root of the dysfunction in Washington.

Some are worse than others due to the divisive tactics they employ. But they are all responsible for this dysfunction. I encourage you to closely watch how they conduct themselves and participate in this failure to serve America.

When I use the word *leaders* for those in congress, I do not mean our leaders but rather that they are the leaders of their respective political parties.

These current leaders have all been in congress for many years, and their leadership positions have changed during their tenure due to which party is in control. The amount of time they have each spent in Washington highlights what is wrong with our national political system.

In the fall of 2015, John Boehner resigned from his office and the speakership, as many challenged and questioned his leadership. Paul Ryan was elected speaker, and we wondered whether we would see any positive change or just the same ineffective status quo!

Well, as speaker, he demonstrated little leadership and simply maintained the status quo with excuses and distractions!

In the 2018 midterms, the democrat party won back the majority in the House of Representatives and Nancy Pelosi was again elected Speaker.

Now after the 2020 election the Senate majority flipped narrowly back to the Democrats with Chuck Scummer elected as the majority leader.

We elect these politicians to office and then assume they will in good conscience form their teams, either in the majority or the minority.

Unfortunately, they have demonstrated their tendency to only allow those in their party who agree with their views to be a part of their leadership teams. This itself creates more unnecessary division. This, along with the fact that many of these politicians have been in political office for far too long, only further complicates the political process.

So, you can see very quickly how within each party we have factions that further divide and only make it harder to find consensus not only within their own party, but as well when dealing with the opposing party and then trying to get an important bill passed and then signed by the president. Political control in Washington is determined by which party holds the majority in each of the senate and house chambers and of course the presidency.

We are primarily a two-party system, Democrat and Republican, with members in both parties holding different viewpoints, such as libertarian, liberal, and conservative, with varying degrees of intensity in each.

Over time, depending on which party has been in control of either the house or the senate, the controlling party has changed the procedural process, which in many cases has created more division and further complicates the entire political process.

Additionally, there are many special-interest groups lobbying congress on a full-time basis in order to persuade members to initiate legislation or to vote a particular way.

These lobbyists are paid by outside groups that want to influence congress and gain access to the process by supporting the reelections of many politicians.

Other factors in our political process are the actions of our president, who can either be a proponent or an opponent of legislation pending in congress.

I would again remind you that President Obama was very much part of the breakdown in our political system simply because he chose to over-politicize every view and action solely to achieve his personal agenda and ambitions.

Our political process was not meant to be any easy process, as our founding fathers understood the importance of passing legislation in the best interest of every American, realizing it would take honest debate and compromise.

However, they realized early on that the human spirit could be corrupted if allowed to act without checks and balances and believed that serving in public office was not meant to be a career choice but rather a desire to serve our nation and its interests.

Sadly, what we have today in Washington are politicians who are more concerned with their reelections and maintaining their power base than we the people.

These politicians have lost their way and no longer serve America, serving only their personal ambitions and believing they are entitled to a lifetime in politics with impunity.

Tragically, they have abused our constitutional system of government and have instituted a corrupt political system with many unnecessary layers of complexity, which they know causes many Americans to simply look the other way!

They use a tactic I like to refer to as political rope-a-dope. Why do I use this analogy? Let me explain.

Remember Muhammad Ali, professional boxer and "the greatest of all time" who introduced the rope-a-dope strategy by laying back against the ropes, covering up, allowing his opponents to punch themselves out, then when they became tired and frustrated, Ali would seize the moment with counterpunch after counterpunch until he won the contest.

So, when I say "political rope-a-dope," I am referring to these failed politicians that delay and distract America to wear us down and then seize the opportunity to accomplish their self-serving goals!

Think about this tactic and how America suffers as a result.

These so-called leaders have so complicated the political process that it is often almost impossible for an important piece of legislation to reach the point where a vote can take place due to endless politicization and polarization, followed by gridlock.

Have you ever wondered why so many times these so-called leaders find themselves at the eleventh hour facing a critical vote and yet in gridlock?

Then they politicize it, such as with threats of government shutdowns or with America unable to honor its financial commitments. They employ this tactic to distract and alarm America in the effort to again complicate the process and further their personal agendas.

Is this leadership? Of course not. It is only politics as usual in Washington!

Please do not believe that they act this way due to principled responsibility to the American people. In many cases, they are only acting to serve special-interest groups who assist them in winning reelection, followed by retaining or retaking power in the house and the senate.

Sure, they must seek and win reelection every two and six years, but for many of these career-minded-only politicians, this is nothing more than a formality.

They have created a political apparatus that ensures their reelection by doing just enough for the respective districts and states, creating the impression that they are doing a good job and are worthy of reelection.

We have to understand that we are somewhat to blame when we continue to vote for politicians only because they bring a certain federal benefit to our local community or state, not taking the time to truly evaluate their real motives.

This is another instance where targeted and silent thought need to be considered, and we need to look at their impact on whether we are exercising our right to vote with critical thought and care for the nation we love.

Please bear in mind that the only thing that politicians do well is ensure their reelection.

These politicians are elected from a local perspective but then as a governing body in Washington are tasked with the responsibility to lead our country in the best interest of all Americans. They disappoint us time and time again and continue to deceive.

We should understand that these long-serving politicians may have come to Washington with interest in serving the voters that elected them and our country, but now only serve themselves.

We are at a time where it has become very obvious that these politicians are human and thus imperfect, and they will continue to seek power if not checked by the American people.

So, we now have to change this system to ensure that we not only correct this crisis in the present but also ensure that it can never happen again.

We are a nation of laws and are granted certain rights under our constitution, which we exercise when we elect our fellow citizens to office and expect them to follow their constitutional responsibility after taking the oath of office.

Many politicians are not remaining true to that oath of office and have lost the trust and confidence of America.

So, is it any wonder that we have lost confidence in our political system?

I know for many readers, the first part of this chapter may seem obvious, and you may agree or disagree with my assertions. If you disagree, I encourage you to take some additional time to reconsider your opinion and please be objective in your thought process.

My goal is to put this crisis in perspective for everyone that reads this book and for everyone to challenge the status quo, what we believe is "normal" in Washington, DC.

This chapter is not only about stating the problems with our political system; it will also provide an achievable solution to this crisis.

That solution can be stated in just two words: term limits.

Now, I know that many will react and remind me that this has been talked about and considered before, and you are correct.

You may also remind me that we do have term limits, in the sense that our president can only serve two four-year terms, and those in congress have to face the voting public every two and six years.

Yes, this is true, but it is not working, and many have found ways to overcome these constitutional restrictions for their own political gain and self-interest.

We must realize that many in congress have decided that they will do anything to ensure they hold office and have now transformed public service into a lifetime career in politics, simply by corrupting our election process.

Let's consider our presidency and former President Obama and if our constitutional term restriction of two four-year terms has been effective.

Have you ever thought about when our president starts to consider their reelection prospects?

It may surprise you, but I believe they are considering their second term while they are running for their first term as president.

Ask yourself, why would they not, especially if they have developed a winning political campaign and organizational structure across America? Why would they dismantle this after winning election and then, if choosing to run for reelection, have to reestablish this all over again?

Why would they not take advantage of the election results that showed where they did not win majorities and then take the next four years ensuring victory in the president's reelection campaign?

They wouldn't, so never believe presidents when they're asked if they will seek reelection and they answer that they have not made up their minds.

This is simply disingenuous, and we should be more alert to this deception and realize that every statement and action that a first-term president makes is guided by a desire to win a second term.

Additionally, we should think carefully about what our president may want to accomplish but will delay until he or she wins reelection and no longer has to face the voting public as a consequence.

So, you can see, the political deception starts early on, and they will do and say anything to win reelection.

Is it not obvious that a president in the first term is simply doing and saying what he or she believes will win reelection and not necessarily acting in the best interest of America?

It should be, but it is amazing how many Americans do not recognize this deception and blindly accept every word, without thinking through it and considering whether there is any truth in these statements!

Think about it. In a president's first term, how much campaigning and fundraising does a president engage in compared to how much actual governing takes place?

So back to term limits for the presidency. In essence, it is very important to limit how long one person can serve as president, as we have witnessed how easily power can corrupt those in Washington. However, we must consider what value there is in having a president serve a second term.

Really think about this! If we believe that a president's first term is very carefully crafted to ensure reelection, then is America really benefiting in those first four years?

Sure, a first-term president is very active and does try to advance political agendas as well as persuade members of congress and the American people to agree and follow their viewpoints.

But are the president's actions in the first term in the best interest of every American or are they only to repay the president's supporters and strengthen those of the same party affiliation?

Please consider former President Obama as an example of why a two-term presidency no longer works in today's political process. Think back to his first campaign for president. Do you remember all the promises of change and unity? What change did he bring to Washington politics?

How much unity did he accomplish in Washington and throughout America?

It is very apparent that this president did not change Washington politics and only made our political system even more divisive and more inept.

With respect to the question of how much unity he has accomplished, he again failed America. As a nation, we have never been more divided, which makes it very difficult to come together as a nation to take back Washington, as I earlier described.

Obama and many other politicians in both parties prefer a divided America, as they know the power of a united America would never stand for their failures.

After Obama won reelection in 2012, did we see any willingness to change politics or bring America together?

Sadly, no!

In addition, we saw a president that decided to sidestep our constitution and issue executive decisions to facilitate his own agenda and personal ambitions.

This lack of respect for our nation and its constitution was even more apparent after his party lost control of the US Senate in 2014.

If this president was honest with the American public during his campaign for his second term about the actions he was planning to take after winning reelection, do you honestly think America would have reelected him?

If your answer is yes, then ask yourself, why did he not express these views during his campaign for reelection?

Search out the audio of President Obama, prior to his reelection, speaking to then Russian president Medvedev, where he was overheard on an open mike, "Please tell Vladimir that I will have more flexibility after the election."

Ask yourself, what was he referring to? Why the secrecy?

And of course, many in our media chose to completely overlook this, yet compare this omission to the distortions and frenzy they perpetuated with respect to Trump. Very predictable!

As a president approaches the end of their second term, many refer to the president as a lame duck, meaning the president in some ways becomes irrelevant or ineffective as they approach the end of their presidency.

So, let's reflect again on the value of allowing a two-term presidency.

Carefully consider a president's first term and how potentially deceptive it can be, not to mention all the endless fundraising and campaigning, and then in the second term all the potential for lawlessness that can go unchecked because the president does not have to face the voters again.

Is this really in the best interest of our nation?

Not only is it not in our best interest but it does little to address the crises we face as a nation.

Sure, our constitution provides for impeachment and removal of our president, but in today's political environment, can we really implement this action?

Not easily, so we find ourselves having to live with the consequences of a failed presidency for eight years and then enduring more valuable time trying to reverse or correct the failed policies of a failed president!

My preference would be a single five or six-year term for the presidency.

I believe that this would limit the potential for abuse of office, distinguish those who truly wish to serve America, and eliminate the need for the deception that a second term naturally produces.

Think about it. We must accept that eight years is too long and that we are not getting any significant value from a president in the first term when they are only concerned with reelection, as I have described earlier.

Then in their second term, we see behavior that was disguised in their first term and a sense that they can violate our constitution with impunity. This, along with their concern for their legacy and not America, only furthers highlights how a second term is not in our best interest. President

Obama's time in office is a vivid example of how two terms can fail to truly serve America.

I want to stress that winning a second term is usually assured and has almost become a formality in today's political system.

We must reshape our political system so that this important office attracts only those who possess a love of country and understand that holding this office is not a means to enhance personal stature but rather to preserve the greatness of America and that of its citizens.

Our president must possess humility and selflessness, not hubris and narcissism, must uphold our constitution at all times, and must never place personal ambitions above those of the American people.

I do believe that after the 2016 presidential election outcome, there were opportunities for President Trump to lead and propel term limits to the forefront of his agenda, but never did.

Do not expect President Biden to ever speak to the need for term limits. However, we should not lose faith in our nation's ability to solve this problem and rise above these disingenuous politicians.

Let's now discuss those in congress and term limits.

I want to stress that the requirement for those in congress to face voters every two and six years does not solve the problem with our political system. Many politicians, especially those in their respective party's leadership, have found ways to win reelection easily.

I believe that having term limits is the only way to address the dysfunction in Washington and that it will fundamentally reshape our political system.

My preference for members in the House of Representatives would be a term limit restricted to five two-year terms, a total of ten years.

My preference for members in the US Senate would be a term limit restricted to two five or six-year terms, a total of ten or twelve years.

So, as you can see, I believe in ten or twelve years in either the house or senate, and then they are out. They will then have to go back to their communities and live under the laws they passed or did not pass while serving in congress.

They could serve in both the house and the senate but no more than ten or twelve years in total. For example, a house representative could serve two two-year terms in the house and then only one five or six-year term in the senate.

After serving a total of ten or twelve years in either the house or the senate or a combination, they could seek the presidency and, if elected, serve the single term.

In this case, it would be a total of fifteen to eighteen years in Washington, and certainly a great deal of positive accomplishments could occur if the person is truly there to serve America and not just to enrich themselves.

But think about this. With term limits in place, is it not more likely that someone would choose public service for the right reason and truly desire only to serve his or her constituents and America? Sure it is!

We must remove any incentives for serving in public office that can result in personal wealth or power; otherwise, we will continue to attract only those of questionable character.

It is very important to understand that just because politicians serve in an office for many years does not mean they are more knowledgeable and therefore would do a better job serving their constituents and the American people as a whole.

For many, the knowledge they gain is how to participate in this corrupt system of politics and nothing else—certainly not how to better serve America.

Too many years in congress only accomplishes the opposite effect. They simply become career politicians with only their careers in mind and not the American people. Many of these politicians have become consumed by the prestige of holding national office.

Those that oppose term limits will argue with great intensity that long tenure in Washington is the only way Washington can work. Not only is this argument ridiculous but look at the lack of results and the gridlock in Washington today!

Consider the records of the current and former leaders in the house and the senate that I cited earlier. These politicians have collectively been in Washington for decades, in both the majority and minority positions.

Ask yourselves, what have they done of a positive nature? Sadly, very little!

But the damage they have done to our political system and our country has been enormous. As a result, America has completely lost trust and confidence in a system of government that was intended by our founding fathers to serve and protect the American way of life.

They have corrupted the greatest constitutional republic ever known to mankind and not for any noble reason but simply to enrich themselves and those who support their deception.

Think about it. We are a nation of well over three hundred million people. Are we to believe that we should accept these same failed politicians year after year and that there are not many Americans who would do a far better job, if not for the closed nature and barriers to entry of this corrupt political system?

Please never be fooled by those who would oppose term limits, especially by those who hold office. They will say and do anything to hold on to their seats in congress and their perceived power. They will target your thought process with deception and try to alarm you that term limits will create unnecessary turnover and chaos in Washington.

Again, utter nonsense!

Turnover in Washington is healthy for our nation, as it will bring new ideas and true patriotism to our congress and presidency. Think about a Washington where our politicians are only concerned with public service, transparency, and compromise. In restricting their terms in office, we are far more likely to see people serve for the right reason rather than serve their personal interests.

I also believe that term limits will reduce the amount of money that has so much influence in Washington. We must remove as much outside influence as possible from our political system. The only influence on our politicians should be the will of the American people.

Special-interest groups provide a great deal of campaign coordination and contributions in a number of ways. This is one of the ways these entrenched politicians are assured of retaining their seats in congress for decades without any real competition.

Oftentimes when politicians decide not to seek reelection, it is due to their desire to take their long political careers along with their Rolodexes and transfer them to careers as lobbyists.

I can assure you that this behavior does not stem from a love of country, only for love of oneself!

I am not objecting to politicians deciding to leave politics and then seek careers to support themselves and their family.

What I am objecting to is a politician that has not served honestly while in congress taking his or her political connections to a lobbying firm simply to enrich him or herself at the expense of the American people.

Term limits may sound like a great idea, but I can assure you that it will not be easy to institute. We would have to amend our constitution, which would have to be initiated in congress or by state legislatures through a state's convention under article 5 of our constitution. Both paths are very difficult and take time.

I would prefer the path through congress, as I believe it would identify the true political leaders and expose those who only seek to abuse their oath of office.

I feel very strongly that as we approach the next congressional and presidential election cycles, if a candidate for president or congress from either political party were to unconditionally accept and promote term limits, this solution would quickly find its way into America's consciousness.

Let me be clear, I am not speaking about a candidate who would only briefly speak about term limits during a campaign stop. With respect to the presidency, I am speaking about a candidate who would not only enthusiastically embrace term limits but unconditionally commit to the American public that he or she would only serve a single term if elected.

Additionally, I believe this candidate would win the presidency in convincing fashion!

Former President Trump, missed an opportunity in his first two years in office, with his party holding majorities in the house and senate, to insist that those in control of both the house and the senate take up term limits and vote yes or no. This would have exposed to the American people those politicians who either obstructed this vote or voted no, which should have resulted in a no vote from America the next time he or she stood for reelection.

Now after the 2020 election results, we have no chance of any discussion on term limits in Washington. However, this could change after the 2022 midterm elections.

If both houses of congress, by each reaching a two-thirds majority, propose an amendment to change term limits, a President Biden could oppose it, but not a problem.

The president does not have a say in this process and can only express his or her opinion. After congress, the proposed amendment would then go to each of the state legislatures for ratification, requiring a three-fourths majority of states voting in favor to amend.

I assure you that this is not an easy process but is extremely necessary at this moment in history. Our politicians in Washington will not do this on their own without a persistent outcry from America.

I can also assure you that if candidates running in primary races for either the senate or the house for the first time embrace and commit to self-imposed term limits if elected, they will win their primary and general elections in great numbers.

Congress has acted to amend our constitution several times in our history, so this is doable, if we find the will as a unified America demanding this of our national politicians.

As much as I did prefer this constitutional amendment be initiated in congress, I really do not believe it to be a viable path given what we are seeing with President Biden and the two Democrat leaders in the house and senate. We may have to pursue a state's convention, so we should be very mindful of our state government legislatures in upcoming elections and which party holds majorities.

The arrogance of Biden, Pelosi and Schumer, is on full display and their extreme policy views and actions could not be more dangerous for America and only destabilizes the rest of the world. Our major adversaries such as China, Russia and Iran could not be happier with Biden winning the presidency over Trump and how weak President Biden has been with their respective leaders and their actions. They now have a willing participant in Biden in their efforts to subvert America.

Another driving force for term limits is to look at how these Washington political leaders so politicized the COVID-19 pandemic that only caused unnecessary harm and suffering for our nation. Not to mention they are pushing more and more trillions of dollars in wasteful spending with no real accountability, with no real concern for America's needs, but again only with political power and personal agendas in mind.

This spending is how those in and outside of Washington get paid. To better understand my last statement, please take some time and look deeply into these spending plans and how much money actually goes to America's critical needs compared to pet projects and those connected to this political corruption in Washington.

I know many feel helpless, but we are not if we take a unified approach to solving this crisis. I am sure there may different ideas on how long these politicians should serve, but the only way to truly rid our political system of corruption and attract the right candidates is term limits!

We also have to realize that two-year congressional election cycles only creates more unnecessary gridlock due to political power struggles to control the house and senate. America truly suffers as a result, as these selfish power struggles only hold back this great nation as it holds us in a constant state of election chaos.

This must be part of our term limits discussion and proposed amendments.

I also know that many do not want to be bothered by this crisis and do not want to spend any significant amount of time thinking or speaking about it.

But think of it this way. Congress and our president should be expected to function normally and in our best interest, but they will not unless we create a framework that removes any ability for these politicians to become entrenched in Washington.

If we just spend the extra time and effort now as a unified America and solve this problem correctly, we can be assured that our political system will function properly without the need for our constant intervention.

As we move to close out this chapter, I want to spend some time on other negative consequences of a political system in crisis. We have seen how unnecessarily complicated and dysfunctional our congress and presidency have become.

A serious concern is that through the dysfunction of those in congress and that of a president, many if not all of our government agencies have become more layered with unnecessary complexity and bureaucracy and are failing to serve America.

Simply put, our federal government has become too large and is now incapable of self-correcting the inefficiencies that exist.

Think back to the two federal agencies I cited in an earlier chapter, the Veterans Administration and Internal Revenue Service.

Especially alarming is when we consider the VA hospital's poor management and the lack of oversight and how it can diminish the quality of care our veterans receive—and in some cases whether a vet lives or dies.

How could this possibly happen and be allowed to continue?

It starts with the president and all the political appointments he or she makes, followed by their ability to manage these appointees.

Then there is congress and its oversight responsibility.

They have both failed horribly with respect to the VA and with countless other examples, and why? Every action has become politically motivated, and every critical decision needed places a political calculation over that of good conscience and the well-being of America.

Another example of a federal agency that became over-politicized by President Obama was our Department of Justice. This is extremely concerning as this agency is tasked with ensuring that even our national politicians are not above the law, or are they? Think about all the federal appointments, such as judgeships, made by President Obama and the extensive damage to America, when a president only makes appointments out of political consideration and nothing else.

Consider the power over every American's life that a president has through his or her constitutional authority to make these appointments and only through a political lens.

The president appoints every federal judge to serve lifetime terms. If our president only appoints these judges based on political calculations and their political beliefs, is this in America's interest?

President Obama did this in great numbers!

Think about the potential for abuse and injustice by activist judges who only rule with a political motive or ideology in mind!

The greatest example of this is the president's power to appoint judges to the US Supreme Court. Look at how politicized this court of nine justices has become.

Almost every decision rendered by this court, irrespective of whether these nine justices have applied our constitution, considering original intent, correctly, is tainted by the political bias of some of these judges.

Congress does have a role in this process as these appointments by our president require the consent of the US Senate. The senate will usually yield without too much opposition to cabinet appointments but will oftentimes hold up appointments to the courts.

Do not ever believe that this process is not heavily driven by politics. It does not matter which party holds the majorities in congress or which party holds the presidency; politics and political bias determine these outcomes.

This process of political appointment followed by congressional oversight is rooted in our constitution, and I am not suggesting that we try to amend this. It can work, but not within this current political system.

However, I do want to highlight how an entrenched political class in Washington, left unchecked and allowed to serve too long, will only abuse this process and prevent it from ever serving America.

Two terms, eight years, for our president is too long and allows too much influence over this important constitutional authority to name political appointees to these powerful positions in both the executive and judicial branches of our government.

With a congress so dysfunctional and so consumed with only holding political power, the ability to oversee these appointments properly and safeguard America from potential abuses that can be taken by those appointed by the president is very much in question.

Effective congressional oversight is further diminished by these agency officials who only obfuscate when testifying before congress.

If through their oversight responsibility, congress finds abuse of office with any of these presidential appointments, they must be prepared to remove these individuals through the impeachment process.

But you see, if congress is incapable of taking this action simply because of political and personal motives and not in honestly performing the duties of their office, then we will be destined to the same failures in government as we have seen with the last several administrations, and for many years to come.

As stated earlier, with term limits for congress and a single term for our presidency, we will change the reason for one's desire to serve America, and I believe that anyone holding power in the executive or judicial branches of government who violates his or her oath of office would be removed quickly by this new breed of politicians.

Before we close this chapter, I want to finish a thought in an earlier chapter on the 2016 Democratic Party's presidential nominee, Hillary Clinton.

During her time in politics as First Lady, US Senator, and Secretary of State, she demonstrated a total lack of respect for the American people through multiple transgressions, dishonesty, and deception.

I would be remiss if I did not cite this one individual as the most vivid example of how bad and how corrupt our political system has become.

Again, ask yourself, why was this person not prosecuted for her misconduct as secretary of state? Are we to accept that this person is above our laws simply because her last name is Clinton and that Obama's corrupt justice department simply ignored these crimes?

This politician, along with her supporters and her acolytes, would do anything—and I mean anything—to win the presidency. They will target our thoughts with relentless intensity and deception.

Please think very carefully before considering this person for any future office or appointment!

In closing this chapter, I would like to remind my readers that patriotism and love of a country in Washington are not values that have been lost forever, but they have been temporarily suppressed by our current political system and can be restored.

When politicians fail, America will fail, unless we act!

CHAPTER 8

American Crisis Number Five—Open Borders and Immigration

What is national sovereignty?

National sovereignty dates to our founding as a nation in the American ideal of independence. Sovereign nations have the right to form governments, enact laws, and defend themselves against those nations that pose a threat to their sovereignty.

When we speak about sovereign borders, we speak about the lines that separate one country from another.

I believe it is very important when discussing this crisis that we keep these definitions in mind and how important these concepts are to the freedoms and liberty we enjoy each and every day.

As with the other crises discussed in this book, this crisis is no different in that it has become just as politicized as every other crisis discussed, possibly even more so.

When we speak about open borders and immigration, I do realize I am stating two separate points, but one is greatly affected by the other.

Let's start with open borders.

As a nation, we have open borders, meaning that we allow immigration for those wishing to come here—but within a legal process.

The open borders I am speaking about in this chapter refer to the unsecured southern border with Mexico, where millions have entered our country illegally.

Fortunately for America, our country is surrounded by oceans to our east, west, and southeast borders. To our north is Canada, who respects the sovereignty of our respective borders.

Unfortunately, along the remaining southern border, we have Mexico, whose citizens and those who cross into Mexico from Central America and other countries enter our country illegally with ease and most certainly do not respect our borders or sovereignty.

We should be clear here. Mexico has been complicit in this illegal entry and does little, if nothing, to restrict this illegal entry into our country. However, during Trump's term and his approach to this crisis, Mexico was much more cooperative with respect to border security.

Mexico has strict restrictions on illegal entry into their country, but their behavior with respect to our southern border is very different.

I want to state very clearly, for those that may distort my assertions, that I am not suggesting that we go to war with Mexico or any other country in the region over this problem.

However, I do believe that America must be very firm with Mexico in solving this problem and exert all the pressure available to us to persuade Mexico to act as a responsible neighbor.

Have you ever wondered why the Mexican government does not do anything significant to assist us or even express a willingness to prevent this illegal crossing?

Let's think about the possible reasons.

Ask yourself, of the people that are here illegally, how many have found work? And where are they spending that income?

Please keep in mind that if someone is here illegally and has found work, it is again illegal on the part of the person or company that hires this person, which is another subject we will speak to later in this chapter.

In some cases, these people are paid in cash, and if so, they are not paying taxes, which is another problem that harms our country.

But where are they spending the money earned? I suggest that the greater amount of this income is sent back to family members or friends in Mexico or other countries of origin.

I would also suggest that many that are here legally through existing laws, such as guest worker programs, also send most of their earnings back to Mexico, but at least this income is taxed. Or is it?

So you see, Mexico is content in not doing anything much to assist us with these illegal crossings of our border and wants as many guest worker visas issued as possible.

This flow of US dollars back to Mexico only helps their economy, so why would they do anything that stop this? They wouldn't!

A second reason may be because Mexico would prefer to see its citizens cross our borders, so they relieve the stress on their public services, especially those who have committed crimes.

Mexico's standard of living for many of their citizens is very low compared to that of America. This, along with the corrupt nature of their federal and local governments, continues to fail many Mexicans.

This same failure repeats itself throughout Central America, so is it any wonder that we have so many desperate people attempting to cross our southern border with Mexico?

One last point on Mexico is its inability to eliminate the drug cartels, who play a large part in the country's corruption. These drugs, in large numbers, continue to enter our country unchecked through our unsecured southern border.

This not only is harmful to the health of our country but also places a great deal of strain and costs on our various law enforcement agencies.

So, let's think back to the importance of national sovereignty and the effect this open border can have.

Would we ever allow a collapse of our US Coast Guard and leave our shores unprotected to invasion by a foreign enemy?

Would we ever do the same with our northern border with Canada and leave that border unprotected?

Of course, we wouldn't! So why in the world do we allow this breach to our national sovereignty and security to continue unchecked with our border with Mexico?

Will it surprise you when I say that it is again political? It shouldn't!

The politicization of this crisis is solely due to the same dysfunction of our national politicians, both Republican and Democrat, as described in earlier chapters. They each have reasons why they want this influx of illegal aliens to continue.

But both parties and their reasons are rooted in politics and not in the best interest of America. We also have a large number of activists who promote this illegal entry and insist on distorting this illegal entry as innocent immigration by those seeking a greater standard of living.

And of course, we have many in the media who distort this crisis to support those who support this illegal crossing into our country.

Your resistance to the targeted thought by others must be at its greatest when thinking through this crisis.

With respect to the open nature of this border, you will hear many excuses, such as "It is not possible to secure the entire border" or "It is not possible to build a wall or fence to secure this border."

This is only deception, which is a tactic used by these national politicians repeatedly to distract America from the real issues and achievable solutions.

Remember my comments on how politicians will over-complicate an issue in order to validate their many excuses for not fixing the problem.

Think about it. This border is approximately two thousand miles in length. Do you not think it can be secured?

More than forty-five years ago, this country undertook the notion to send a man to the moon, and in 1969, an American took the first steps on the surface of the moon.

This vision and belief in America's greatness was initiated by JFK, a true leader. Sadly, our current and recent Presidents did not possess this type of leadership ability.

So, are we to believe that with today's technology and American ingenuity, we cannot create a secure wall or fence, whether it be physical or virtual, along with increased border agents where it might be necessary in some stretches of this border?

Without a doubt, we can, and we could do it very quickly.

Americans know this and have become frustrated with our national politicians, especially during the Obama years, and his lack of willingness to act in America's interest.

President Trump did have the determination to deal with this problem and did take steps and initiated action to secure this border. He was able to start construction of the border wall with hundreds of miles completed by the end of his term,

Mr. Trump projected strength and purpose when dealing with Mexico on this crisis, getting Mexico to act as a more responsible neighbor.

However, the same dysfunction in Washington, as discussed in the last chapter, tried to deter any lasting solution to secure this border.

Now after several months in office, President Biden has only worsened this crisis to a state not seen before. Not only did he stop the border wall construction, but rescinded effective policies instituted under Trump, such as the remain in Mexico pending asylum hearings.

Make no mistake, we have a silent invasion of this border taking place, meaning those rushing across this border are not doing so with guns blazing but are still invading our country.

Some may believe that the word "invasion" is an exaggeration of this problem. It is not!

These people that are crossing our border are infringing on every American's right to a secure nation. Those crossing are also seeking to take advantage of America's freedoms, public services, and opportunities.

These freedoms and benefits belong to every American and those here legally and not anyone else, regardless of their plights. We must resist the temptation to think of this in only a humanitarian way and not as the true threat that it is.

Additionally, we look foolish and weak as a nation to the rest of the world in our ineptitude to secure this border.

It is only a matter of time before those who truly wish to kill Americans find the way to exploit this open border and do great harm to our American way of life. This may have already occurred, with these terrorists now rooted in America and simply waiting for the right opportunity to kill in great numbers! Do not be fooled by those who understate the possibility that this can occur. It is already happening when you consider the extent of drug and human trafficking that is taking place with ease across this border.

Also, we know many of these people crossing our border are criminals, guilty of serious crimes, such as murder and rape, and sadly, they have committed this same type of violence against innocent American citizens.

So again, with all of this said, why are we not securing this border?

How can the greatest nation on earth allow this to happen?

It is due to the incompetence of the same entrenched politicians we spoke of in the last chapter. Without the correct political will, this problem cannot be fixed.

Every American must demand that this breach in our national security be corrected immediately and loudly express disappointment at every opportunity—and certainly at the ballot box!

In the prior chapter, I spoke about candidates running in the upcoming election cycles embracing and self-imposing term limits and how successful those candidates would be in winning their respective offices.

If those same candidates would also commit unconditionally to secure this border, he or she would bring even greater certainty to winning.

It is essential that we secure this border and treat it with the same security measures and importance as our other borders. This must be done before any honest discussion or compromise on immigration can take place.

In the Trump presidency, border crossings were down sharply because he allowed our law enforcement agencies at this border, to simply do their job.

We must remain committed to securing this border's entire length through a fence or wall and settle for nothing less!

Now let's discuss the second point of this chapter, immigration.

As we discuss it, it is critical that we inform ourselves on how serious a crisis this is and the serious consequences of allowing it to continue without change.

Let's try to take the emotion out of our thought analysis for a moment, which is why I stated earlier that this crisis is probably more politicized than the other crises talked about in this book. By emotion, I do not mean compassion or concern when thinking through immigration.

However, with only emotions, and without clear and fact driven thought, we will continue to allow the overpoliticization of this crisis to distract America from the true nature of the problem that confronts us.

It is important to understand that an open border with Mexico is simply a means to ensure an end-result that many politicians use to accomplish their goal of unchecked entry into our country.

It is also important to understand that former President Obama and his Democratic Party and those who support it, along with many in the media, distorted this American crisis. The Republican Party also distorts this crisis but not in such a divisive way.

I believe that the Democratic Party believes this unchecked entry of illegal aliens will lead to a reliable voting bloc and a way to deceive American citizens of a Mexican or Latino heritage that the Republican Party only wishes to discriminate against them and those wishing to immigrate here.

I also believe that some in the Republican Party look the other way on this crisis, with the intent to appease business donors that look to this illegal entry as a means of cheaper labor.

While I do believe the Republican Party is just as responsible as the Democratic Party for not solving this crisis, I do feel that there are some in the Republican Party that are honestly trying to find ways to secure this border and deal with immigration in the best interest of America.

By some, I am not referring to the current leaders in the Republican Party that only give lip service when speaking to this problem. These same entrenched politicians in both parties have not only politicized this issue but overcomplicated it as well.

Additionally, over the eight years in office, President Obama chose to not enforce many of our immigration laws and instituted unlawful immigration measures through abusing the executive order power of the presidency.

I would ask you to consider the following question very carefully. Are our Washington politicians, including Biden, really concerned with the well-being of these illegal aliens?

In fairness, I must also state that former president George W. Bush was also very weak on border security and immigration.

They are simply using these people as a means, to a political end with interest only in their own agendas and ambitions and certainly not with any great humanitarian concern.

However, in their attempt to deceive us, they distort their comments and attitudes to appear as if they really care about the human element to this problem.

Remember the recurring statement "This is not who we have been as Americans" that many say when trying to convince Americans that they are on the correct side of a crisis, when in reality they are only trying to target and influence our thought through emotion and a twisted view of patriotism.

America cannot be the America we love and cherish unless we place Americans first. It is that simple.

We must be honest that, yes, these are fellow human beings, but crossing our border at will violates our national sovereignty and therefore is illegal.

This illegal action is threatening the well-being of America and every American citizen, as well as noncitizens who are here legally and that have followed our immigration laws.

So, let's stop with all the distraction, distortion, division, and emotion and discuss this crisis in a pragmatic, honest, unified, and calm way that produces an American solution.

This crisis further highlights the need for America to take back Washington and rid ourselves of the corruption that is eroding our political system, limiting our ability to deal with this issue.

Let us now think about the causes that encourage and allow illegal entry into our country.

First and most obvious is the unsecured nature of our southern border. This is as if we had a great beacon in our southern sky that shouted, "Come on in whenever you like!"

So yes, let us do what is best for America and secure it now!

Our immigration crisis is not only caused by the openness of our southern border but also by other failures.

As mentioned earlier, Obama chose to ignore many of the immigration laws already in place. He used his executive power to unlawfully change the status of many illegal aliens that are here, allowing them to come forward without the fear of deportation.

This is nothing more than an attempt to find a pathway for the millions of people here illegally to bypass our lawful immigration and naturalization process.

The goal of Obama, now Biden, their party, and other supporters is to bestow the right to vote on those that have crossed our border illegally, which they believe will create a reliable Democrat voting bloc.

Obama's executive orders on the DACA and DAPA initiatives have been challenged in court, some aspects blocked, followed by review by President Trump. Who knows where President Biden plans to push these initiatives.

So, there has been no leadership coming from Washington on this crisis. The actions by Obama and now Biden and those that supported them served only as a catalyst for those who wish to come to America—that they can do so illegally and without fear of deportation.

Please remember, as I have pointed out in earlier chapters, that many of our politicians, including former President Obama, prefer a state of crisis and confusion when confronting the challenges that face America.

They believe a crisis makes it easier to deceive and alarm America, which allows them to advance their policies quickly and without adequate debate and analysis.

They are not interested in what every-day Americans think about this crisis. As always, they are only concerned with their own personal agendas and ambitions.

In many cases, their deception only widens the crisis and pushes the proper solution further and further from reach.

I do believe that President Trump looked at border security from an "America first" perspective, but I am not sure he truly saw immigration in the same way.

He has changed or not fully clarified his position on those here illegally at different times during his presidency.

Our southern border states have tried various measures to stop the illegal crossings and limit public services to those here illegally but have been blocked by the federal government time and time again.

Immigration falls to the federal government for policy and enforcement, so if ignored by those in Washington, it only creates greater chaos and stress for those bordering states.

Every tax dollar that a state spends on immigration enforcement, in instances where the federal government should be enforcing laws, not only puts undue stress on a state's budget but should make us wonder what is happening with our tax dollars to fund these various federal agencies tasked with immigration enforcement.

I do not believe that anyone truly knows the number of illegal aliens in our country at this time, but we usually hear between ten and twenty million. It is likely much higher, but even if it were just ten million, is that not very alarming?

Those here illegally are not just huddled in place and hiding in our southern border states. Many have moved or been relocated by our federal government to different states across America. Many states and cities have wrongfully created sanctuaries with incentives that attract many illegal aliens.

This only creates more confusion and barriers to our local authorities' willingness to work with federal immigration and enforcement authorities to properly address those here illegally.

Many states offer taxpayer-provided services to those here illegally, such as public assistance and education. Our health care delivery is also used by those here illegally.

All these benefits are simply free, meaning that those here illegally are not paying taxes and therefore should not be entitled to any assistance and benefits. It only rewards their lawlessness.

Remember my earlier mention of those here illegally who are violent criminals. Not only does this unnecessarily threaten our safety but think of the tremendous cost to prosecute and incarcerate these criminals!

This is further highlighted by the instances where violent criminals, after committing violent crimes, serve time and then after being deported simply walk back across our border and again commit violent crimes in this country.

In some cases, this happens multiple times by the same person!

All of this creates unnecessary strain to these states' budgets and continues to raise the taxes for Americans and those here legally.

Many states are struggling to balance their budgets, and many Americans are suffering as a result of an overburdened condition within their various state agencies, which only they should be entitled to!

Don't you find it ridiculous when you hear those that support this unlawful entry into our country make foolish statements such as "This is the right thing to do" and "How could we look the other way when there are so many children affected?"

What about America's children and the children of those here legally?

Throughout this immigration debate, we hear more and more about the term "anchor babies" and the Fourteenth Amendment to our constitution.

This discussion is of course distorted by many politicians and those who support illegal entry.

The term "anchor babies" refers to the children of illegal aliens who are born while they are in this country illegally. These children are considered legal residents at birth by those who wish to stretch the rights established in the Fourteenth Amendment.

These same politicians and those who support illegal entry also believe that these babies born to illegal alien mothers within US borders are called anchor babies because, under the 1965 Immigration Act, they act as an anchor that pulls the illegal alien mother and eventually a host of other relatives into permanent US residency. We have many in politics and those that self-describe as constitutional experts interpret the Fourteenth Amendment differently and are driven by varying political views.

I will not attempt to convince anyone that I am a constitutional scholar, because I am not. However, as an American citizen, I have read this amendment and listened to the various arguments on both sides of this debate.

I do not believe this amendment guarantees the rights of citizenship to babies born of those here illegally.

The real contention is over the words in section 1 of the Fourteenth Amendment that states, "all persons born or naturalized in the United States, and subject to the jurisdiction thereof, are citizens of the United States and the state wherein they reside."

I strongly encourage my readers to spend time reading and understanding not only the amendment itself but the amendment's authors and their rationale for proposing it. They also clearly stated at the time that it did not include those born here of illegal aliens.

Please also consider the wrong it was trying to correct when adopted back in 1868.

I would also ask you to take notice of those who disagree with my assertion and that of many Americans in how they craft their deceptive statements to promote their beliefs that the Fourteenth Amendment does grant citizenship to those born here of illegal aliens. They would have you believe that we are acting as radicals in defying our constitution and should seek to amend it rather than oppose it.

This is the same distraction and deception they regularly use to accomplish their personal and political agendas without any concern for a true American agenda!

This amendment does not need to be changed; it simply needs to be applied properly with American wisdom.

Lastly on this subject, the US Supreme Court has not ruled on this matter specifically, but some have tried to distort and state that it has ruled specifically on this issue.

However, if it did come before our US Supreme Court, one can only imagine how they would rule, given how politicized this court has become.

I did not want to spend this much time about anchor babies, but it is very important to see that it does create another incentive for illegal entry into our country.

I believe it highlights the absurdity of those who argue that the acceptance of anchor babies is legal and good for America.

As we continue to examine our country's immigration, I would like to stress that those who always speak to "comprehensive immigration reform" and feel it should include those millions currently here illegally and securing our southern border are wrong.

We should not have to consider and debate new laws or changes to existing laws because our leaders have failed to safeguard our sovereignty and have not secured this border or quickly deport illegal aliens before they can root their way into American communities.

When those who support illegal entry into this country speak of comprehensive immigration reform, what they really mean is ignore the border, allow continued illegal entry, quickly legalize the illegal aliens already here, and pass legislation to expedite naturalization of those same people.

This is a disingenuous approach and should be rejected, as including border security is only a ploy to deceive America that they are we really concerned about this unchecked and unlawful entry into our country. They are not!

We should not believe for a minute that, with current state of political dysfunction in Washington, a comprehensive immigration reform type of approach is even possible, but most importantly it is not necessary.

It is so obvious that the correct path and first step is to immediately secure this border with a permanent structure and, while doing so, deploy the appropriate amount of manpower in border patrol enforcement and as well as our National Guard in the areas most prone to illegal crossing.

Think back to Mexico and their resistance to assist in restraining this illegal entry and ask yourself, how much in foreign aid do we send annually to Mexico and Central American countries? For example, on average, we give Mexico tens of millions in aid annually. Why would we continue this unless they cooperate fully with us to restrict this unlawful entry?

We should cut this off immediately unless they continue to act more responsibly.

We should also consider trade restrictions as well, unless or until Mexico does more to act as a responsible neighbor.

Trump did push back on these countries in relation to aid and trade with success by including this in his negotiations.

The frustrating aspect of this crisis is that, with the current political leadership, it is almost impossible to have any real change and honest debate. Now with Trump out of office and Biden in, we are falling back into the same weak posture which existed prior to Trump.

However, if America comes together and insists that congress act to secure this border now, we may see some results. But we must speak so loudly that those standing for reelection in 2022 and beyond realize that if they do not act now, they will not receive anywhere near the majority of votes to retain their respective offices.

This is why I stated earlier that a candidate running for national office must not speak to this crisis broadly but speak very specifically, loudly, and repeatedly about the need for congress to act now on securing this border rather than wait and continue to make excuses. I want to state again, I believe the Republican Party is just as responsible as the Democratic Party for this crisis, but I do believe that some in the Republican Party have expressed genuine concerns regarding immigration as well as border security.

We must expose those in congress who ignore the need to secure the border and only offer the same tired excuses. Congress can and must appropriate the funding needed to finally secure this border.

In 2006, the Secure Fence Act was passed to secure seven hundred miles of this border, yet less than one hundred miles was actually secured with a double-layer fence, which was the original intent of this act.

Examine closely any claims of a greater number of miles that are secured, as our government includes vehicle barriers and inadequate fencing in their current estimates of how much of the border is secured through fencing.

Former president Obama froze the development and deployment of the virtual fence component of this act. Any surprise?

Donald Trump did hold the Department of Homeland Security and its secretary responsible for border securement. He also started and completed several hundred miles of a border wall, but it was immediately suspended by Biden after he took office. Again, no surprise.

The American people must now watch this process closely and punish those who vote no or those who skip or try to block future votes, with a no vote for all of those seeking reelection.

We need new leaders who will challenge these entrenched politicians in both political parties in the house and the senate in the upcoming primary elections for their offices.

Simply stated, enough is enough with this issue of border securement.

The number of illegal aliens currently here is not only due to the openness of our southern border. We have many that overstay their nonimmigrant visas, such as those for tourists, temporary workers, and students.

The length of time allowed to stay varies among the different types of visas issued. We also issue border crossing cards for those crossing from Canada and Mexico.

Additionally, we allow entry for those from countries where we participate in a visa waiver program for those traveling as tourists and for business.

The actual number of those overstaying these nonimmigrant visas and other programs is not known. However, it does vary based on the type of visa or program.

Government and research groups' estimates vary, but you often hear that between 25 and 40 percent of those here illegally have over-stayed their visa or other border crossing programs.

When you closely listen to why this is happening, you hear over and over again that we cannot adequately match entry and exit of those holding visas, so we cannot be sure who has overstayed and is now here illegally.

You also hear that this is not so much of a problem for those traveling here by air and sea but is much more of a problem for those crossing our land borders, and the length of stay allowed also creates problems in tracking these visas.

This failure by our government to control and prevent overstays is just as ridiculous as our inability to secure our southern border. After the 9/11 attacks, we found that several of the hijackers had overstayed their visas.

Supposedly, this was the wakeup call for government to act and implement a state-of-the-art system to match entry and exit for all those that held legal status to come here on a temporary basis.

This has not happened, and again, it is due to the incompetence of those in Washington and their desire to follow other agendas instead of an American agenda to solve these problems.

Think about it. With today's technology, such as biometric identification and the ability to quickly transmit data via the internet, it should be easy to accomplish a reliable system of matching entry and exit, if we have the will!

Also, if we had this system fully in place, think about how easy it would be to identify those overstaying their visas, if we implemented biometric identification at certain points where those here illegally try to gain access or benefit from America or when interacting with law enforcement.

This would not infringe on our liberty and freedom as Americans, as this initiative is only to identity and match those IDs of those here illegally if they were registered properly through bio-metric identification when first entering this country.

It should be unthinkable that the greatest nation on this planet and with supposedly the brightest minds in IT cannot solve this problem.

Ask yourself, if a system of government is failing and harming America, would you allow it to continue and accept excuse after excuse, or would you simply shut it down until it is fixed?

My desire would be to temporarily suspend and limit immigration until this is resolved. Sure, I know immediately that those who support illegal entry would loudly shout about the harm it would cause and those that rely on tourism from other countries would object. I am not suggesting limiting our tourism industry.

However, tourism was sharply curtailed during the Covid pandemic, think about it.

But think about the harm and cost to our nation by not addressing all immigration including the number of refugees allowed to enter each year!

Again, my intent is to limit immigration and slow it down until we have an immigration policy in America's interest, not in the interest of those wishing to come here.

We must put America first!

Immigration should be a means to enhance a country's prosperity, not diminish it—and certainly not putting the interests of those wishing to come here over those of American citizens and those currently here legally and seeking naturalization.

America has nothing to be ashamed of with respect to immigration and our generosity, as we have for several years issued on average each year one million resident visas (ten-year green cards) and we naturalize nearly the same annually.

The fact that America is the most prosperous and freest nation in the world is not a reason to allow endless immigration, and we should not allow anyone or any group or any other nation to demand different of us!

Another concern and reason for slowing immigration is to allow for the proper assimilation of those that have immigrated here legally, which is absolutely critical to America's future. It will keep this country America and not let it become a large mass of subsets of other nations without any national unity.

We must realize that the greatness of America is at risk if we allow immigration without the necessary assimilation that adopts American values and beliefs, which is the only way for America to replicate its greatness for generations to come.

The percentage of those here who are foreign born compared to those US born is rising. Think carefully about this. Is this healthy for America? We must be very thoughtful and remember that America's greatness is rooted in the loyalty of its citizens to America and no other nation.

The "melting pot" analogy when describing our society can only work if we have proper assimilation, unity, and a true desire by those immigrating here to adopt American values.

Yes, each of us has a proud heritage, and we should not forget that many of our parents and grandparents emigrated here from countries around the globe. But our hearts and minds must belong to America, which creates American patriotism, which is like no other nation in the world!

Along with America's great freedoms and liberty for its citizens comes a serious challenge, as with these freedoms, we easily allow illegal aliens to root themselves in our society, and unless they engage in criminal activity, they are not easily identified as being here illegally. Ask yourself, why do many of our state and federal agencies provide documents and instructions in not only English but Spanish? Is this not helping many of those here illegally from Latin America to continue unchecked and unjustly take advantage of America's greatness?

Of course, it is. We should stop it and insist that English be the only language with respect to our state and federal governments and not facilitate those who choose not to learn and accept English.

As I stated earlier, each of us are very proud of our individual heritage, and many of us speak more than one language, and that's fine, but if you wish to come here legally and become an American, the only acceptable language is English.

We know that a majority of those here illegally are of Hispanic descent. We also know that those of Hispanic descent that have resident status or those who have been naturalized comprise a growing percentage of the US population.

Therefore, we must be very vigilant when thinking about this and the potential damage it can have on the American fabric. Closely listen to those in favor of this unchecked entry across our southern border and their eagerness to legalize and naturalize those here illegally.

My concern is that we may be undergoing a silent invasion right before our eyes by those who wish to change America and refuse to assimilate to our culture and values, choosing only to embed their culture and values into American society!

As we close this chapter, I want to spend some time on another incentive to those who wish to violate our sovereignty, most specifically those coming across our southern border.

The incentive is that many now know they can find work, even if here illegally, as many US companies, small and large, will hire them.

Again, this is the result of our federal government's incompetence and failure to act responsibly and leverage American technology and ingenuity.

I am sure many of you have heard the term E-Verify along with the I9 form, which are meant to verify employment eligibility to legally work in the United States. While E-Verify has had success, it still has problems with employers adhering to its use and other disconnects.

I do not believe we have a lack of technology solutions but rather a lack of political will to enact and then enforce the solutions. Additionally, we have an underground economy in our country, meaning we have company and individual employers paying their workers in cash and not reporting their wages or paying related income taxes. This is just another incentive for those to cross our border illegally, and it makes it easier for those who knowingly hire those here illegally to operate their businesses.

As much as this is illegal on the part of these employers and does harm to our country and should be corrected, we must also recognize that our government makes it very difficult for small businesses to survive.

Please consider the large number of Americans and those here legally that are unemployed. You may have heard of the labor participation rate, which measures the number of people sixteen years and older who are able to work. It has fallen dramatically. It now has stabilized and started rising after the election of President Trump but must be watched and considered very closely.

In 2020 and 2021, due to the COVID-19 pandemic, this economic indicator did suffer. However, as we move forward, Biden's policies will cause this metric to fall or stay flat. The national unemployment rate also improved under Trump. I still believe this indicator is far from accurate, and this metric continues to be distorted by our government.

Our poverty rate, as well as the number of those on public assistance in one form or another is still very concerning.

Think about these alarming facts very carefully! Why would we even consider immigration of any sort until we address the employment and social needs of America?

Don't be fooled by those who distort these facts and say there are many Americans who won't perform the work available and therefore those jobs are taken by those coming here legally as well as illegally.

These are the same people that promote limitless government and state dependency programs that do not provide any incentives or pathways for those unemployed or in poverty to lift themselves out of this endless cycle of despair.

Ask yourself, why we would continue these same policies regarding our immigration strategy when it is obvious that this country cannot continue to absorb the high numbers immigrating here legally? When added to the high numbers of illegal aliens, it will only continue to erode America's prosperity.

After the great surge of lawful immigration between 1880 and 1920, in the period between 1925 and 1965, we did limit immigration into our country.

Look at the positive results of that pause and how those that immigrated here during this surge period successfully assimilated into America—and then how those born here of those same immigrants created one of the greatest generations in our nation's history.

Just like with other crises talked about in this book, you will have to be on guard to recognize all the distortion and distraction by those in politics and the media who have no interest in solving this crisis but only in pursuing personal or political agendas.

You may have noticed that throughout this chapter I have only referred to those here illegally as "illegal aliens," not as "illegal immigrants," not as "undocumented immigrants," and not as "citizens in waiting" or any other ridiculous politically correct reference.

The solutions to this crisis are very simple, but our politicians, activists for illegal entry, and those in the media who support them will dispute this assertion and will only complicate this crisis, which is an all-too-common tactic they use to deceive America.

As I have stated before, I firmly believe in American correctness and the wisdom of America to solve this crisis, and I encourage my readers to embrace their important role in solving this crisis.

America, please step forward, as we must solve this crisis!

CHAPTER 9

Now What?

Great question—but one that has many answers!

First, when considering this book and its value, please do not do so with only emotion. When considering our current state of transition and crisis, we must remain calm, think critically, and consider not just our own individual needs, but America's needs as well.

If we allow those who wish to change America's fabric and core values to advance their agendas, America will falter and the impact to every citizen would be devastating!

Consequently, the world as we know it would suffer, so it is vital that America unite and reject those who wish to divide and diminish this great nation.

Have you ever considered what is in your *thought toolbox*? Let me explain.

We process thoughts in many ways, as we discussed in chapters 1, 2 and 3, and then how our thought process affects our perspectives and actions.

Our thought toolboxes can be very basic, meaning that we just allow our thought process to occur without any real examination of what is causing the thoughts we have, and then form our opinions and actions.

Conversely, some of us possess thought toolboxes that are much more discerning, meaning we apply varying degrees of analytical examination of what enters our consciousness and the thoughts it creates, which of course guides our actions that follow.

I encourage each of you who possesses only a basic thought toolbox to upgrade your toolbox to one that will enable you to apply more examination of the thoughts you process.

This upgrade will not be the same for everyone, and I am sure some will say they do not need any change in their thought analysis. You may be correct with respect to many of life's daily experiences, but when considering the major crises facing our nation, and certainly, the ones I cite in this book, you will need an upgrade.

The upgrade I am speaking of is nothing more than a conscious decision to find the time in our busy lives to consider our thought process and these crises in a way we have never done before.

We must find the catalyst that will convince us that we need to rethink how we prioritize our thought process and then allocate sufficient time to reach objective thought and outcome.

I hope this book and the crises discussed will help to provide that catalyst.

Please keep in mind the focus on politics in this book and how we process all the incoming political news and often just accept it as factual. We must understand that there is little fact in most of the political news we encounter.

This is not only due to a great bias in many of our news outlets, but as we have discussed in this book, our political system, especially at the national level, is corrupt and unworthy of our trust.

Ask yourself when you feel the most informed. Is it when you simply listen to others and their opinions, or is it when you search out your own sources and answers and then form your opinions?

I believe that most of us would state the latter.

We do this every day, some more than most, in varying degrees. However, when it comes to politics and by extension the management of our country, we all too often don't.

So, a vital part of your thought-toolbox upgrade is to ensure you consider politics on a much more frequent basis. Let me also stress that many of us who possess complicated or highly technical thought toolboxes may need upgrades as well when considering the politics of our nation.

After reading this book, I would encourage you to strongly consider your approach to thought and politics and then read this book a second time.

My goal is not to convince you to allow politics to consume every aspect of your day but rather to convince you to take a more pro-active role in our country's politics and the governing of our nation.

But we must choose the right leaders!

Our constitution grants us our right to vote. As we age, we should never forget the enormous leverage this provides to us and never, absolutely never, fail to exercise this right and privilege!

Additionally, we should never underestimate the value of this single vote when we are considering whether to participate in the election process of a public official or any other ballot issue.

Remember, those who seek to influence our vote with deception and dishonesty would rather we not vote at all, if they cannot be assured of our vote in favor of their agendas.

For those of us in despair and unable to find meaningful work, please do not cast your vote for any politician, either local or national, who promises to give you more assistance if you vote for him or her. This may sound convincing, considering your personal circumstances, but in reality, your vote for these politicians will only continue to grow government and make you more invisible to these same dishonest politicians!

Ask yourselves, as the government continues to grow, which it has dramatically, why haven't the levels of poverty and unemployment evaporated?

These same politicians try to convince us that if they raise taxes on companies and those individuals at higher income levels, government will then help those of us in despair.

The truth is that the more the government taxes, the larger it becomes. It will only continue its wasteful spending and nothing more!

Sadly, our local and federal governments fail to even find the ways to ensure our safety in many of our neighborhoods and communities, which is the result of these same failed politicians!

The larger government becomes, the smaller America becomes! Please understand that waiting for the state and federal governments to provide benefits and doing nothing else will only hold us in place and not provide any opportunity for us to grow and move out of poverty and despair.

Our current government does not provide opportunity, only dependency!

The only way we can lift ourselves out of poverty is through hard work and personal responsibility, which will provide us with a pathway to greater prosperity.

That awful job we take today may be very difficult, but we should use it as the motivation to work even harder, which will enable us to find that next great job that will propel us forward and allow us to fully participate in America's greatness.

So, I ask those who find themselves in poverty to resist this tendency to vote for those who only make promises and seek to grow government and to instead consider those who inspire and seek to reduce government.

This also applies to those who are working and supporting families, those who are living paycheck to paycheck, or those who do not feel they can accomplish much more.

For those who feel they are doing well or are growing families, experiencing many of life's pleasures, and having great jobs and good incomes, they too must resist the tendency to vote for big government.

Those doing well may not truly understand that many of our fellow Americans are being left behind and falling into an endless cycle of poverty and crime because of a dysfunctional government that will not change unless we force it to change.

Our government in Washington is consumed with politicians concerned with their personal enrichment rather than enriching America!

I implore every American to understand that we are in a very important transitional period due to the triggers and events I spoke to throughout this book.

We are poised to reverse these errors and eliminate the threats since the start of the 21st Century that placed America in a state of crisis and uncertainty.

We must insist that President Biden does not take us in the wrong direction that continue these risks but rather follows the path that continues America's greatness that will safeguard our freedoms!

However, as discussed Biden has not demonstrated any willingness to preserve America or safeguard our freedoms and has only demonstrated a very partisan and a very radical ideology.

We must act now to persuade our elected politicians in Washington to understand that unless they pursue an America first agenda, that we will punish them when they next stand for re-election.

Please take the time to review our nation's history and how we transitioned through difficult events that threatened our freedoms. We are not a nation of simply disconnected individuals but rather a nation of shared principles and purpose that demands a coalition of every individual who chooses to be an American!

During your review, I respectfully ask my readers to do the following.

First, read our US Constitution and the 27 amendments that followed. Please pay special attention to the first 10 amendments (The Bill of Rights) as well as the Preamble. I encourage you to memorize the "Preamble" which will allow you to easily apply this short, but very succinct rationale for our constitution, when evaluating our Washington politicians and their actions.

Next, read our "Declaration of Independence". Please pay special attention to the part that states the following.

"We hold these truths to be self-evident, that all men are created equal, that they are endowed by their Creator with certain unalienable Rights, that among these are Life, Liberty and pursuit of Happiness. That to secure these rights, Governments are instituted among Men, deriving their just powers from the consent of the governed".

I again ask my readers to memorize this powerful excerpt and apply this when evaluating our Washington politicians and their actions.

Please reflect on the very last statement of this excerpt "deriving their just powers from the consent of the governed". We must never allow these entrenched politicians in Washington to forget this condition of holding the office we elected them to and that *We the People* are in charge!

Yes, I know, we all have our hands full with all of life's challenges, but please take more time to carefully consider whom you are voting for and why.

I can assure you that if we take these initiatives in the short term, we will solve these crises and reestablish a government for its citizens, which will be immune to the corruption we see today.

These actions will free us from having to deal with it again and allow every American, and I mean every American, to enjoy the greatness of this nation.

We must enact term limits, reevaluate these short election cycles and settle for nothing less.

We must speak so loudly that our voices will shake the halls of congress and send the message to these failed politicians that their days in office are truly numbered.

I find myself finishing this book over the Memorial Day holiday which honors our fallen military in the many conflicts fought to secure our freedoms which really highlights the need for us to solve these crises and not allow those lives lost to be in vain!

We must successfully navigate through this transition, solve these crises, and continue America's journey!

I would like to be able to title my next book, *The Spoken Thought: America's Comeback*!

ABOUT THE AUTHOR

Charlie Wurz is a freedom-loving American seeking to understand what promotes thought or the lack of thought as well as why thought is not always expressed through words or actions. This is his second book. In this book, Charlie furthers the discussion from his first book. Not only does he expand on the major crises facing today's America but also identifies the transitional period that was triggered as we entered the twenty-first century and major political events over the last twenty years.

Charlie lives and works in the Washington, DC, metropolitan area and has serious concerns for America's path forward. He expresses these concerns as American crises providing thought-provoking analysis and commentary.